The View from Cracker Hill

The View from Cracker Hill

Bettejane Synott Wesson

Copyright © 2008 by Bettejane Synott Wesson.

Library of Congress Control Number: 2007907576
ISBN: Hardcover   978-1-4257-8437-9
           Softcover   978-1-4257-8409-6

All rights reserved. No part of this book may be reproduced or transmitted in any form or by any means, electronic or mechanical, including photocopying, recording, or by any information storage and retrieval system, without permission in writing from the copyright owner.

This book was printed in the United States of America.

To order additional copies of this book, contact:
Xlibris Corporation
1-888-795-4274
www.Xlibris.com
Orders@Xlibris.com
40480

To my sister. Wish you were here.

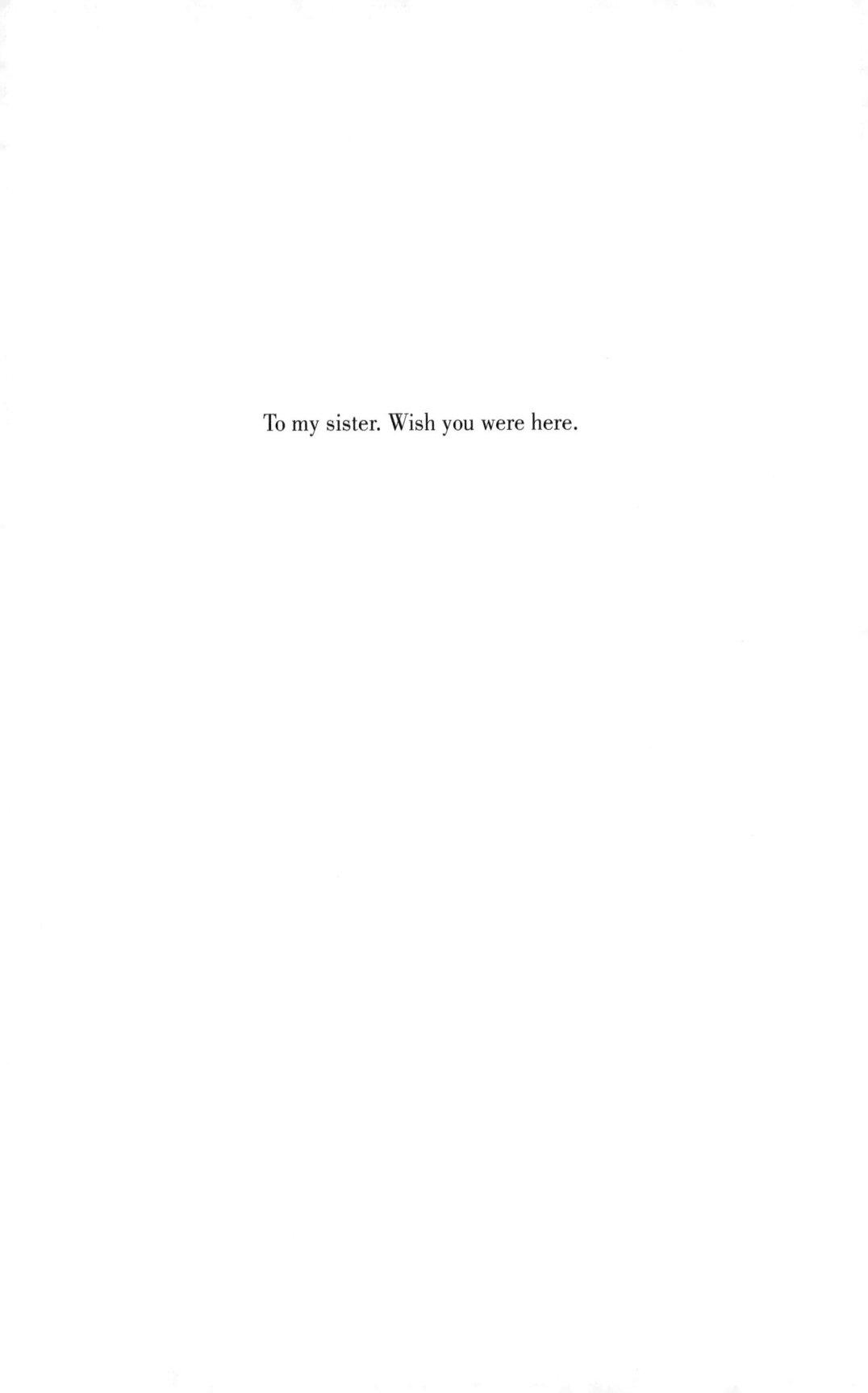

Table of Contents

page 9   Introduction
page 11   Our Neighborhood
page 21   Our House
page 33   Our Family
page 36   Downtown
page 71   School
page 77   Horses
page 81   Around Town
page 97   Flood Friday
page 103   Christmas
page 113   A New Year

Introduction

Waterbury, Connecticut, is a city set alongside the banks of the Naugatuck River and connected by bridges from east to west. If you happened to be driving across Connecticut on the highway corridor called Interstate 84, you'd be afforded a panoramic view of what was once hailed as the Brass Capital of the world. Waterbury's area spans 28.2 miles. Waterbury's industrial heyday spanned a century.

During World War II, in my parents' time, the brass industry was at its peak, churning out defense products. But the postwar economy began to tell a different story. Flood Friday in August of 1955 did away with large sections of neighborhoods along the Naugatuck River, and the urban redevelopment that paved the way for I-84 through the heart of Waterbury continued the job of changing the city's face forever.

Some people welcomed the highway as progress and the way to make Waterbury the crossroads of New England on the twentieth-century map. Yet somehow, the creation of this east-to-west route bisecting Route 8's pathway north to south made the city a place to pass over rather than a destination.

But Waterbury was built to last. Just like its legendary locally made Timex watch described by John Cameron Swayze in his 1950s TV commercials, the Brass City could "take a licking and keep on ticking."

From both highways, you can see the key features of Waterbury's face: Riverside Cemetery tucked beneath Route 8, the gold dome of our Cass Gilbert-designed city hall, the twin gray stone spires of Saint Anne's, the French church in the south end. Off I-84 in the east end is the Brass Mill shopping mall, built on the site of the old Scovill Company's brass factory.

Dominating the Waterbury sky is the 240-foot red brick tower of the Union train station, now home to the Waterbury *Republican-American* newspaper. The building was commissioned by C. W. Mellon, president of the New York, New Haven, and Hartford Railroad to be his company's flagship station. Its tower is modeled after the bell tower of the Palazzo Publico in Sienna, Italy, and was designed by the firm of McKim, Mead, and White.

Flowing along from north-to-south parallel to Route 8, the Naugatuck River winds sedately, tamed by the United States Army Corps of Engineers after the devastating flood of 1955. You might enjoy slowing down for a good look at the city as you drive along, particularly if you're a Waterbury native. From the highway's bird's-eye view, you can see how all of the city's neighborhoods, which can seem so separate when you're driving on its streets, fit together to form the big picture its citizens call home.

North of the train station and its dazzling tower, Willow Street begins its gentle rise uphill from where Meadow Street meets East Main. From the highway, you might glimpse the beige stone bell tower of a church through the trees. It's St. Margaret's Church, just two blocks above the house where I grew up. Willow Street is said to have taken its name from a tree, long gone, that stood in front of a Dr. Johnson's house at the corner of Johnson and Willow.

It was a pretty name for a street lined with grand old houses, and I liked it better than Cracker Hill, a term I'd heard applied to our part of town. Local lore held that the people who had built here had been reduced to eating crackers as a dietary staple after putting their last dimes into paying the bills for turn-of-the-century grandeur.

That story never explained the term to my satisfaction, but I accepted it as a kind of fable, knowing that there was always more to everything that met the eye. I grew up on stories told to me by family members and read to me at night before I went to sleep. My story is about the way Waterbury looked to me when I was growing up on Cracker Hill in the 1950s.

Our Neighborhood

My mother's mother loved to walk. Perhaps it was because she'd grown up in Ireland in the countryside of the Lake District. Walking was how you got around in what Grandma referred to as the "old country." There were bicycles too and jaunting cars; but it was the rare person who had an automobile, according to Grandma, who had an endless supply of tales about Killarney's green beauty, its lakes, and leprechauns. It sounded like a nice place to visit, but it was clear to me that she preferred Waterbury's city sidewalks and the convenience of the green and cream-colored CR&L busses that ran so regularly from her part of town to ours.

Grandma arrived by bus at our house several times each week, and in good weather, we set out on foot after lunch. Our route took us down Willow Street past the yellow stucco Bernard Apartments, where my best friend lived three floors up by creaking elevator. A turn to the left and we were on Hillside Avenue.

Hillside curved gently like a dowager's necklace around the gently sloping hill. In this necklace, the jewels were the mansions set up from the sidewalks on wide green lawns. Gracious verandas wrapped around their fronts. Porte cocheres depended from their sides. Quirky peaks and gables decorated their roofs. Down on Cliff Street stood a brick mansion converted to a convalescent home, the one house I'd actually been inside. My class had gone there one Christmas to sing carols to its residents, and the high-columned entrance crowned with a carved cornucopia above the massive front door had awed us.

On the north side of Hillside, the mansions were set high with long sidewalks or steps up to them that made them seem to be built nearly in the sky. I was enchanted with these houses and longed to go inside. We never saw anyone on the porches or lawns, so I imagined their secret lives. I pictured paneled dining rooms and chandeliers, roast goose at dinner served on silver platters. I felt certain that the ladies of the houses retired each night to their boudoirs to lounge in peignoir sets on chaise longues and comb their long blonde hair.

My fantasies about life on Hillside Avenue were fed by my reading material. I read constantly, daily, the way some people smoke or eat. I devoured books. At ten, I'd left fairy tales behind and moved on to the world of Dorian Gray and the adventures of Sherlock Holmes. It was the ambiance of the English country house that I envisioned behind the closed doors of this part of Waterbury.

In the fall, the gardeners of the mansions raked the leaves from the lawns into tepee piles. Fanning out across the slopes, they then swept the piles to the sidewalk curbs to await pickup by city workers. All the children in the neighborhood waited to jump into those leaves when the job was finished to bury ourselves alive in the dry, crisp, earthy smell of autumn.

In winter, the shingle-style house that commanded the corner of Hillside and Kellogg allowed sledding on its front lawn. It was thrilling to glide to a halt just short of the street, to swish down and turn the red metal runners of my Flexible Flyer at the last possible moment. In the background on sledding afternoons, the gardener hovered watchfully, his shadowy figure reminiscent of Mr. McGregor observing Peter Rabbit at play in his cabbage patch.

But it was in warmer seasons, not winter, when Grandma and I took our walks. If we turned right off of Hillside and down Pine, then left along the narrow lane called Glenridge Street, we came out into the open space of Hayden Park. A Victorian mansion known as Maplewild had been razed by the Hayden family and the land donated to the city. Hayden was a park for passive recreation, so there were no basketball hoops or playground equipment. But what there was, in the center of the flat smooth lawn was a wide shallow wading pool made of concrete. The cement was the same composition that formed the oval walk around the lawn's perimeter.

In summer, the fountain at the pool's center shot jets of water into the air. It fell on the heads and shoulders of the children crowded beneath it. In the bright sunlight, the concrete, mixed with tiny pebbles and bits of mica, sparkled as if set with diamonds.

If I'd come with my bathing suit on beneath my sundress, Grandma would wait on one of the green park benches while I splashed decorously along the pool's edge. I waded out into the center only on days when it was uncrowded. I hated being shy, but despite my family's pep talks and my own resolutions, shyness proved as resistant to change as my all too obvious freckles.

The neighborhood children and I went to different schools. I was downtown on Church Street at Notre Dame Academy, an all-girls Catholic school. They went either to Driggs public school on Woodlawn Terrace or to St. Margaret's parochial school behind the church on Willow. My school friends lived in other parts of the city and play dates with them were highly unlikely since my mother did not drive. Then, too, my mother wasn't keen on friendships with the kids on the block, so summers found me reading on the front porch in the shade of the green striped awning or playing with the cats, and my long walks with Grandma when she came to spend the day were a welcome diversion.

On days when our walk continued after the park, we'd turn back up Pine Street. Leaning into the steep hill, I could feel the muscles in the backs of my calves pull. I liked to pretend I was on an expedition to climb Mount Everest, no mean feat of imagination on an August afternoon.

When we reached the shady expanse of Columbia Boulevard, we slowed our pace. This section of town, planned and laid out by Henry Cables in the early 1900s, was called Overlook. A wide grassy median strip separated the Boulevard into two one-way streets running north and south. Planted with shade trees, the center strip was a little park in itself. At intervals in its plush lawn were carefully tended flower beds, the plantings changed from geraniums to chrysanthemums by the park department according to the season.

All of the houses were big, and most were painted white. Doctors and lawyers made their homes in this part of Waterbury. Shiny, wood-paneled station wagons were parked in their driveways, a practical conveyance for families that ran to five or more children each. Lawns of them in color-coordinated playclothes, and the occasional maid in uniform watching from behind a screened front door completed the picture. These houses matched the description of those in the town of Riverdale where my idol Nancy Drew, Girl Detective, lived with her lawyer father and their faithful housekeeper.

I imagined Nancy on this street, perhaps in the corner house with the front porch swing. No doubt she'd be inside, as she often was, "in a brown study," on their davenport. I had only a sketchy idea of what a davenport was, but it seemed likely that the brown study was the room where they'd placed it.

When I was grown-up, I planned to live in Overlook too. And as Grandma and I walked, we played a game of choosing which house would be mine. Although the style of architecture was mostly colonial, each house was unique, and all were beautiful. Deep porches and the occasional tile roof in the Spanish manner, one house with a columned portico like an illustration for the cover of *Gone with the Wind*, gave the street a hushed ambiance that made me want to whisper, and I looked forward to passing one house with stained glass squares in its front entrance, a playful wink that seemed to say not to take it all too seriously.

At Roseland Avenue, we went left toward Willow if I couldn't convince Grandma to turn onto Clowes Terrace and the secret staircase that led from Sand Street onto the bottom of Tower Road. I liked its big steps, surrounded by a tangle of trees, and the unusual back view of the multifamilies that turned their faces toward Willow.

Grandma, though, preferred the long way, past the red brick Engine 6 firehouse at the top of the hill. Firemen in short-sleeved shirts sometimes stood outside the building on hot days. I'd peer inside to see if there might be a Dalmatian somewhere and always hoped for a fire call to answer the question of whether the men really slid down a fire pole from the second floor when the alarm sounded.

"Nice day today," they'd say as we passed. Grandma always answered with a gracious nod, her face shaded by her flowered hat of summer straw.

Below the firehouse, Willow Street was multifamily homes and mostly triple-deckers—a style of house as characteristic of Waterbury as the clock on the Green, the Carrie Welton Fountain, or the train station's brick clock tower. Waterbury was a factory town, and these were houses where its workers lived.

The porches on the fronts of these wooden buildings were graduated in size in the same way as the three bears' chairs in *Goldilocks*: a big one for the first-floor rent, a middle-sized one for the second floor, and a tiny one for the third floor tucked beneath the eaves of the broad peaked roof.

I'd imagined life inside the houses we'd passed on our walk, but in these houses, I knew what life was like. Cousins, aunts, and uncles lived in similar ones in other parts of the city. The kitchen was at the heart of things here. There'd be a linoleum floor and a white porcelain sink with lumpy legs, a stove on one wall, and a refrigerator on another.

On the wall behind the stove was the round hole where the old stovepipe had vented out, covered with a metal plate that looked like a dish, and was painted to match the wall. Unless the occupants had remodeled, there were no kitchen cabinets. But most rents had a spacious pantry with cupboards and glass doors handily located by the back door into the room. The most modern of housewives boasted fifties' chrome and Formica kitchen sets, the tables and chairs gleaming like the tail fins on a showroom Cadillac.

Cooking smells rose and mingled in the back stairwells of these houses, cabbage competing with marinara sauce, reflecting the city's ethnic mix. An ironing board and iron set up for business, a line of flapping laundry outside, a radio tuned to AM talk show WATR all added to the picture.

At the corner of Willow and Ludlow was our church, Saint Margaret. It was a church in transition—"growing up," as our pastor reminded us. Next to our small yellow Mission-style stucco building, a new church was beginning to rise. It was built of pale brick and was to have bronze doors and marble floors.

Every parish home had a cardboard container shaped like a brick. On its side was a drawing of the new church. On top of the box was a slit labeled My Weekly Donation. The box said, "Give back to God for what he has given you." Rays fanned out from the church spire illustration, so that it seemed to beckon.

When no one was around, I liked to rattle the box. My weekly contributions of a quarter were making it heavier, and each box, when filled, was said to be the equivalent of one real brick. Could I choose exactly which brick would be mine? Inspired by the famous sidewalk in Hollywood where the stars left their hand and footprints, I hoped so, but was told that it was highly unlikely.

Holding down the corners of the city blocks on Willow were stores. Some were in brick apartment buildings, but others were in triple-deckers on their converted ground floors. I counted a package store, some drugstores, a few barbershops, and several markets. At the very bottom of Willow on the east side lay the Wilfred Beauty Salon. In its window was a huge vase of ornamental grasses—their tall dusty-looking plumes dyed red and amber, blue, and green. I looked forward to seeing them each morning on the way to school and imagined them to be like the bulrushes where Moses had been found by the pharaoh's daughter.

Dead ahead on West Main Street was an apartment building that had a monkey in one of its upper windows. I couldn't tell if the monkey was alive or stuffed although I studied it carefully at every opportunity. It was as exotic to me as the flora in Wilfred's window. Over and over, I'd ask my father why the monkey was there and if it was real, but his answer never varied from "who knows?" said in a tone of disgust.

Across from our house, the block was anchored by drugstores, Keefe's at the corner of Hillside and Delaney's at the corner of Ridgewood, where we caught our bus downtown. Keefe's soda fountain was the place to go for a vanilla Coke or an ice cream soda, usually concocted by the druggist himself in his white lab coat. Delaney's had a selection of cards and a little window in back where we bought our stamps from the druggist's daughter.

Once, my grandfather sent me there for a birthday card for a friend. I chose one with a rose-covered cottage flanked by doves underneath a heavenly blue sky. Unfortunately, I'd neglected to read the message. I'd selected a sympathy card and was sent back to explain my mistake.

Traffic on Willow was brisk, and I was never allowed to cross the street without adult supervision, so my solo excursions were always on my side of the street. But I also noticed that even when I walked with Grandma, we never ventured down the streets on the west side. Except for Brick City, the apartment building on Johnson where one of my dad's aunts lived, that area of town was a mystery.

Two doors up from our house was Dave's Superette—a handy melange of canned goods and Sunbeam Bread, cold soda, and fresh meat. Dave's was also my mecca for comic books, handily located on a rack inside the door. We didn't have a freezer, so a daily trip to Dave's for suppertime ingredients was de rigueur.

Down in back on a sawdust-sprinkled floor in front of the meat locker, the white aproned butched wielded his cleavers over a wooden chopping block. On occasion, as he filled an order, he'd down a glistening piece of raw liver. This was an amazing feat and one I never tired of watching.

Around the corner on Ridgewood, any time from 5:00 p.m. on, on summer nights, mothers called their children home to supper as grown-ups disembarked from the Reidville-Overlook bus on their way back from work. Later on those hot nights, the neighborhood's porches filled with people out to catch a cooling breeze. They leaned against the railings of those tall multifamily wooden houses like travelers on ocean liners bidding, "Bon voyage."

One summer afternoon as I was reading on our front porch, a gray sedan pulled up and parked. Inside were two men, sweltering in suits and hats like the ones Dad and Grandpa wore to Mass. The men sat there all afternoon. Next day, they came back. My mother studied them from behind the living room curtain, then came out for a closer look.

"I'll tell the police. They may be up to no good," she called upstairs to Dad's mother. But in fact, the two men were the police on a stakeout for someone who was thought to be staying across the street. A few of the houses there had been converted to rooming houses, where people lived for a while and then moved on. In one house a year or two earlier, a woman had killed herself, stopping up the cracks around her window and doorframes with bedding and turning on the gas.

When my mother found out that the two men were plainclothesmen, she brought them glasses of lemonade. We took wild guesses at what the man they were looking for had done. It was good to know that we lived in a city where the police were Johnny-on-the-spot in protecting us from the criminal element.

Some arrests were published in the newspaper, and there was one crime in particular that caught my eye. It was called "lascivious carriage," and its perpetrators were always women. When I'd asked my father to define it, he'd paused a moment, then replied, "Lascivious carriage? That means they were walking funny." For someone who walked as much as I did, up to confession on Saturday nights, and often to school or to the library, this definition was a new source of worry and one more reason to be self-conscious. How would I know if I was "walking funny?" But though I pressed Dad for more details, that was all the information I got.

I wondered if this walking-funny business might include something I saw occasionally across the street where the tavern's Open sign winked an inviting eye. In warm weather, its door to the dim interior stood open night and day. From our front porch, we had what Dad called ringside seats to whatever went on in the neighborhood.

Once in a while, someone's exit inspired Grandma to sing a song whose chorus went something like this:

> The doors swing in, the doors swing out,
> Some pass in, and others pass out.

In Saturday cartoons, the characters who drank saw pink elephants, and I wondered what the tavern patrons would have thought if they'd chanced to glance out the open door the afternoon Priscilla, my calico cat, escaped from the doll carriage and ran down Willow Street in a red satin doll dress and knitted cap.

What we drank at our house was tea; pots of it simmered to inky darkness on the gas stove in an old warhorse of a teapot with a curving spout. Often the paper tags on the tea bags caught fire, but one of us simply blew them out. With our tea, we favored jelly donuts from the Brooklyn Bakery, though my grandmother upstairs could be counted on for a homemade cake or pie for Sunday's dinner and perhaps later on, as well.

Tea at my mother's parents' house came with Royal Lunch milk crackers slathered with butter and jam. Sometimes Grandma patted together a soda bread. It amazed me that in spite of using never using a recipe, the bread came out the same every time—rock hard. She told us it was how they ate it in Ireland, though we remained skeptical. Still, it was studded with currants, and she'd made it, so we considered it a treat. Teatime was about conversation and family, and in Waterbury, there was never a lack of either food for thought or of topics worthy of discussion.

Below our house on Willow just beyond the corner of Hillside lay the funeral parlors, a dignified use for the big Victorian houses. Long canopies imprinted with the establishments' names stretched over their front walks. Black limousines gleamed in their backyards. And on nights when there was a wake, solemn men in dark suits held open the heavy front doors for mourners to pay their respects.

As I saw it, the funeral parlors were directly linked to politics, a favorite topic of discussion in Waterbury at any time, from the beauty parlor to the dinner table. I knew that the Snyder Funeral Home belonged to a Republican who sometimes served as mayor. The Bergin Funeral Home on East Main Street across from Crosby High was owned by Democratic Mayor Bergin, who lived two blocks above us on Woodlawn Terrace. It seemed to me that the two took turns at running the city, and for a long time, I believed that being an undertaker was a requirement for being mayor of Waterbury.

Although I did not know it at the time, the houses on Cracker Hill and the Hillside mansions were as connected as my hand was to my arm. What connected them was brass. At the end of the eighteenth century, Waterbury's landscape was still rural. But by the middle of the nineteenth century, engravings of the city showed a change to smokestacks towering above the houses, belching smoke. It was a time when blackened skies meant prosperity rather than pollution, an opinion that continued through my growing up. There was even a local joke that you could tell what day of the week it was by the color of the Naugatuck River. It varied according to what factory was discharging its waste. An iridescent river was as matter of course as the days when a south wind blew up from the valley bringing with it a taste of Naugatuck's pungent rubber shop hard at work.

Yankee ingenuity began Waterbury's industrial career with the humble button—first of pewter, then of brass. When manufacturers found a way to roll brass rather than fashion it by hand, the city was on its way. It helped that there was so much water around to power machinery and that there was seemingly no end to what could be made of brass. Unskilled workers came in droves to the city seeking jobs, and between 1850 and 1860, Waterbury's population almost doubled.

All along the rivers, the factories grew, south on the Mad River and the Naugatuck and north on Great Brook. Sometimes old sawmills or gristmills were converted into factories for making buttons or clocks. The city grew as well, getting its first bank in 1848 and its own branch of the railroad in 1849.

Just like the "begats" in Genesis, many of the brass companies were interrelated. Augustus Chase, president of Waterbury Manufacturing, was also president of Waterbury Watch, Waterbury Buckle, and Waterbury Pin. There was plenty of room to spread out and give each item made its own factory.

Back then, Waterbury's Hillside section was still country, high enough to catch a cooling breeze, and with a great view of the growing city. The industrialists headed there to build their houses, and when they built, they built to last. The exuberant Victorian style of home was in vogue with the occasional sprawling shingle cottage, the English manor house, and the Tudor. But no matter what their style, one thing all the mansions had in common was size.

Below them, around the Green, Waterbury's streets wore the manufacturers' names: Scovill, Benedict, Porter, Coe, Hayden, Leavenworth, Goss, and Chase. Just as the Hillside belonged to the brass fortunes, the lower Willow Street area belonged to the bankers and lawyers, doctors, and insurance men who served them.

As the city grew, Willow Street extended up the hill from West Main. Its middle section was filled with three-family houses, many designed with fanciful turrets and gingerbread-trimmed porches that echoed their Hillside neighbors.

At the top of Willow, sloping down toward Waterville beyond the firehouse, the street made a gradual transition into twentieth-century architecture. Colonials stood next to houses in the Spanish Mission style, Arts and Crafts period dwellings alongside Tudor revivals. This section of Willow shared boundaries with Waterbury's exclusive Overlook section, designed by Henry Cables and built on top of Burnt Hill.

As the middle class scaled Cracker Hill toward the new "best" section, their old homes on lower Willow became apartments, some with office space on the ground floor. Prosperity meant moving up, houses included. My family had come to Willow Street in 1949, from the Brooklyn section of Waterbury, sharing space in the first house my parents and Dad's parents had ever owned.

Our house was a small single family, dwarfed by its triple-decker neighbors. An elderly neighbor whom my mother often visited told us she'd been born in our house in an upstairs bedroom, so we knew it had been on Cracker Hill close to one hundred years by our time.

The first floor, five rooms and a hall, was ours. Upstairs were four rooms for my grandparents. A bath in our former pantry, a sink and stove installed in the second-floor back bedroom, and the house was divided in two. But the walnut-banistered staircase connected us and kept us on an intimate footing.

In my grandparents' bedroom at the top of the stairs, two of the windows faced south. From them, when the leaves were off the trees, I could see a few smokestacks. And in the morning, when I lay in bed, I could hear factory whistles blowing their wake-up call.

My hometown, Brass City, made products that touched the world. Maybe it was just a snap or a shoelace eyelet, a pin or a watch, but chances were good that whatever state in the Union you called home, you'd have something on you that was made in Waterbury.

The town was filled with factories, and yet it seemed that the only ones who knew what went on inside them were their workers. Our grammar school class had toured an apple orchard in Bantam, and my Girl Scout troop had visited the city's sewage treatment plant, but although Waterbury was turning out everything from hinges to hairpins, all I ever saw were the finished products.

I had an inkling, from watching a Saturday-morning TV show called *Industry on Parade*, of fast-paced assembly lines and metal stampers, rolling mills and machines the size of trucks. And I knew for sure that the work was hot and dirty.

Sometimes, driving out Hamilton Avenue to visit my mother's parents on a hot summer night, we'd see the men on Scovill's night shift leaning out the windows of the factory to catch a little breeze. Their cigarettes glowed red against the dark sky, their dark-streaked faces were indistinct as they looked down on the passing cars.

Every home I'd ever been in had local factory products, Chase chrome ashtrays in the parlors and Hamilton Beach mixers in the kitchens. Our sewing kits were Dritz, and our belts had Waterbury buckles. Then, too, there were the brass tubes and caps my great-aunt made at Scovill's in our peacetime economy.

"Lipstick cases," she told me, though to me they looked suspiciously like converted bullet casings.

Out of all of Waterbury's products, my favorite one was clocks. My mother's father had worked in a clock shop for a while and could repair them, so interesting out-of-town ones like a Forestville clock and a Winsted-made Gilbert clock of brass with four glass sides had found their way to my grandparents' rent on Rawley Avenue. But at our house, except for a Waterbury pendulum wall clock, the products were brand-new. There were Big Ben alarm clocks and kitchen clocks in plastic cases shaped like animals or cartoon characters such as the schmoo from Al Capp's *L'il Abner*.

U.S. Time, the old Waterbury Clock shop, had contracted with Disney to make watches with cartoon characters on their faces. Some were Mickey Mouse, but for mine, I chose Cinderella. The factory had a program where you could sign up to be a watch tester. You'd wear the Timex for a while, fill out a questionnaire, then send it back, and get another one in a different style.

Down on Johnson Street, three blocks below our house, Lux Clock was turning out timepieces like Grandma's new one, in an uneasy marriage of brass and plastic. Called the pendulette, her tiny clock was molded to look like a Swiss cuckoo one carved of wood. When its pendulum swung to-and-fro, the little metal bluebird at the top swayed, keeping time.

Waterbury didn't know it then, but those clocks were harbingers of the future. Plastic had begun to replace many of the odd-sized parts that its factories had for decades stamped out of rolled brass. The machines that made those parts were out-of-date, and so were the big brick buildings that housed them.

Factory workers had fought for and won better working conditions: safe environments, higher wages, shorter hours. Strong unions gave workers the power to strike. On occasion, Dad's father would be summoned to pin on his AFL-CIO button and head down to the union hall for a vote. So while in history textbooks labor vs. management was a black-and-white equation, in Waterbury, those workers were family and neighbors and friends.

They were the man across the street missing fingers where he'd caught his hand cleaning a roller at "the shop," as people called the factories where they worked, and the woman we knew who worked at an old-fashioned machine with shackles attached. She fastened herself to it each morning, she explained, so that the handcuffs could yank her hands out of harm's way if the press came down too fast.

This kind of work was how they made their living, and they'd tell you that they understood that the bosses "had to make a buck" too. But here and there, changes were beginning. Some factories were closing down completely or moving south to build new plants in places where they could hire cheaper labor.

For Waterbury—the city whose motto read, "Quid Aere Perennius?" ("What is more lasting than brass?")—change had come from a direction it would not have supposed. It had sprung from its own brass roots.

Our House

198 Willow Street was the address our mail came to each morning. It was delivered by a mailman with the same last name as ours, though no relation, pushed through a brass slot in the bottom half of our green front door. The top half of the door was glass, with a white lace curtain that filtered its western view of sunset, scattering the light into tiny gold lozenges onto the walls and floor.

The envelopes slid with a swish onto the front hall carpet, a runner vivid with pink cabbage roses on a gray background. The rug continued its journey up the stairs and along the second-floor hall to my grandparents' part of our house. I liked our house divided. It provided both an extension of my world and a different one, conveniently attached.

Everything about our house seemed remarkable to me: the closets deep enough to walk around in, the bathtub with clawed feet, each one wrapped around its own iron ball, and the long windows that opened onto the side and back porch roofs. Most intriguing was the wall safe in my grandparents' bedroom just above the radiator.

I saw it open once, when we went with a real-estate man to see the house for the first time. I was surprised at how small the inside was in comparison to its round metal face. After the house was ours and I asked to look inside, Grandma told me the combination had been lost.

Whether or not that really was the case, her story put an end to my requests to open it, though not to my speculation on what might be inside. I imagined an Ali Baba treasure of jewels left by the former owners and never tired of spinning the knob on its dial on the chance that I might hit the combination.

My grandparent's bedroom at the top of the stairs had a long multipaned window that looked out into our horse chestnut tree, a tree that always sent its best specimens onto the porch roof rather than the lawn where I could collect them.

Between the two south-facing windows was Grandma's mirrored dresser—its drawers full of sachet scented slips and nightgowns, lace-edged hankies, and a tiny pillbox with a red jewel in its lid. Centered on the cutwork bureau scarf behind the gold-tone mirror, comb and brush set was a china Madonna and Child, whose clasped hands held Grandma's wedding band each night for safekeeping.

Grandpa's bureau was where he kept his Purple Heart and Oak Leaf Cluster, next to a pile of handkerchiefs ironed with their initial *S* showing in the top corner. To me, the little quilted satin boxes of gloves and handkerchiefs, the veiled hats and fitch fur piece in Grandma's bedroom were the marvelous toys of a grown-up woman that I could play with every day.

The only drawback to her room was between the twin mahogany beds with pineapples carved on their finials. It was a crucifix as long as a yardstick, and it dominated the north wall, both by day and in the darkness too when Jesus glowed softly in phosphorescent green.

Across the hall lay the living room, its length achieved by joining two former bedrooms. Our television was there, positioned, though not intentionally, so I could view it from the top step after I'd been tucked in downstairs for the night. Sitting quietly on those stairs in the chilly dark hall, I glimpsed the grown-ups' world as it was presented on TV.

The snippets of shows stayed with me as dramatic background music and canned laughter. There were two standouts: one where the dancers formed a pattern like a kaleidoscope as they lay on the floor kicking while filmed from above and another where couples danced to an orchestra while a machine blew bubbles into the air around them. But the one I couldn't forget was an advertisement for batteries that made it hard for me to sleep later as I recalled the ominous lines of them marching in formation down a deserted street.

What I liked best about the second-floor bathroom was the full-length mirror on its closet door. Slightly hazed with age, it gave a murky reflection that made even my school uniform look attractive. The kitchen accounted for the rest of the second floor. It was where my turtles lived in their plastic bowl complete with plastic palm tree. Their island was filled with tiny multicolored pebbles with a pearly glow. The turtles' backs were painted with orange marigolds, the sides of their busy little heads naturally striped in a clash of green and yellow.

Amazingly enough, they subsisted on dried ant eggs shaken from a little cardboard can. Since the best part of Grandma's kitchen was her baking, I pitied them for their peculiar tastes. As for me, winter afternoons often found me on Grandpa's platform rocker, my feet on the oven door of the gas stove, opened for an extra blast of heat. My after-school snack was a slice of Grandma's cake, perhaps the white cake with mocha frosting. As I ate, I could contemplate the gold-rimmed decorative plate above the range. It showed Jesus and the apostles chatting over bread and wine at his Last Supper.

Grandma's pies were even better than her cakes; the pineapple cream and the lemon meringue were my favorites because of their toppings arranged in peaks. There were only two food items that I fled from: liver, which not even its accompanying bacon could make palatable, and a concoction my dad called by the name he'd used for it in the navy to describe a melange of chipped beef, white gravy, and toast.

Downstairs in our part of the house, our rooms were larger and more public. The room to the left of the hall was our parlor. Two front windows faced Willow Street and were long enough to step out of onto the porch if we had cared to. Across from them, french doors led into an inner room, perhaps a library in a past time. Now it was my parents' bedroom.

Their mahogany bedroom set was waxed to a finish that reflected me nearly as well as the dresser mirror. My mother's white leatherette jewelry box was centered on her bureau. Dad's had a mahogany crucifix on the wall above it that was really an emergency device for Catholics. Optimistically it was called the "sick call" set, but it was really for the last sacrament, extreme unction. When you unscrewed the crucifix from its base, a tiny coffinlike cavity held a candle, holy water, blessed oil, and whatever else the priest might need to send the departing person on his or her way in a state of grace.

There was a glass bottle of holy water beneath it on the doily that matched the one on Mom's bureau. This was used mostly for thunderstorms. At the first rumble, my mother would head for it and go through the house sprinkling it to keep us from being hit by lightning. I never questioned the ritual. It made as much sense to me as placing our statue of the Blessed Mother in a window facing out if we needed the next day to be sunny, or taping a dime to the base of the statue of the Infant of Prague to ensure we wouldn't run out of money.

Statues seemed more reliable to me than praying to someone invisible. I'd tried it once on my mother's recommendation, with mixed results. I'd developed warts on my left knee, and my mother had advised me to pray to Pope Pius XII, who needed a few miracles for canonization. Less than a month later, running down Baldwin Street to a birthday party, I'd tripped and skinned my knee. As she cleaned and bandaged it, my mother remarked, perhaps hoping to cheer me up, that my prayer had been answered.

"The warts are gone now," she pointed out, failing to notice my stricken reaction to the heavy-handed help I'd so thoughtlessly invoked. Asking for assistance from an unseen presence in the great beyond was something I felt reluctant to try again any time soon.

The only holy object in our kitchen was a discreet cross over the back door, fashioned from the palm we got each year on the Sunday before Easter. Like all of our rooms, the furniture here came in a set, the maple table and china cabinet of early years giving way to fifties' chrome and yellow Formica.

Furniture came from Hampson, Mintie, and Abbott or Hadley's. Rugs came from Howland-Hughes and curtains from the Windsor shop. Like our living-room couch and chairs, curtains were selected for their own merits rather than their ability to coexist with wallpaper or with anything else in the room, for that matter. Each part of the decor—the flowered drapes, ivy-laden wallpaper, checkered tablecloth, bookends of little Chinese children in coolie hats—contributed to the rooms I called home. And if I'd been a philosopher, I might have drawn a parallel between those rooms and the eclecticism of Cracker Hill.

My dad and his father were handy. I grew up thinking that all men knew how to fix things. In fact, since they always let me help them if I asked to, I also supposed I might have a genetic predisposition to be handy myself. In our kitchen, the knotty pine paneling halfway up the walls was done by them, weekends and evenings after work. Painting and papering, hanging light fixtures, even building stone walls in the backyard, and sewing the awnings for our front porch, all were done by Grandpa and Daddy.

What I liked best about the knotty pine was the little faces in its knotholes. There was a particular one by the water pipe in one corner of the kitchen that looked like a grinning elf. It was just to the left of our wall phone. Our house had only one phone number, Plaza 51864. Anyone could answer the phone, and everyone did. If it was for my grandparents and we had picked up, we'd bang the receiver on the water pipe that led to their kitchen to alert them. If Grandma had answered on their extension, she simply "yoo-hooed" down the stairs.

In our kitchen, the linoleum was inlaid in a pattern of blue wreaths on a background of dusty rose. The grooves in its design made the floor a pip to wash and wax. That was Dad's project every Thursday night, "swabbing the decks" as he put it. It seemed as if our house should have glowed with all the cleaning that went on. Summer mornings found my mother hosing the front and back porches and sweeping the sidewalk, and the breezes that blew through the open windows never got a chance to take the starch out of the ruffled curtains, they were changed with such frequency.

Beyond the organdy tiebacks of my bedroom window lay the back porch, its railing a favorite perch for our two cats. The canned food they ate smelled so overpoweringly fishy that we fed them there on the opposite side of the door from us. By day, the cats lolled in the sunshine, but by night, unless shut in the cellar, things were different. There were certain times of year, referred to by Dad as "cat time," when the neighborhood cats gathered in our backyard and howled. Our cats, Cynthia and Priscilla, were the pets I dressed in doll clothes and bonnets. I had even baptized them with a generous splash of Mom's holy water so they could join us in heaven. Naturally, I wanted to see what those nights of bloodcurdling yowls were about. But my parents disagreed, and my bedroom shade stayed down. I had an idea that the cats' business had something to do with the sixth and ninth commandments, vaguely described in my Baltimore catechism as "impurities." The other commandment in play in this situation was the fourth, obedience to parents.

For someone who usually had to invent a few venial sins to satisfy the priest behind his confessional lattice on Saturday night, three broken commandments would be the sin jackpot. I imagined a roar that would flap the maroon velvet confessional curtain and be heard as far away from Cracker Hill as the Green. And so the cat situation became one more discovery to be made when I grew up.

My bedroom on my side of the partition that Dad had made to give my sister and me each a private space had a bureau, a Hollywood bed with a padded headboard, and a vanity table with a ruffled organdy skirt. Its stool meant that you could sit and admire yourself in the mirror with sculpted leaves on its oval frame.

I was nowhere near the makeup stage; but I liked the glamour of my mirror, comb and brush set, the tiny bottle of Houbigant perfume in its lumpy white hobnail milk glass container, and the little hidden drawer in the vanity that held my barrettes. Dad had built a bookcase into the partition, and on it, I'd arranged my collection of books. Nancy Drew and Judy Bolton surrounded my eighteen-inch-tall plaster statue of the Infant of Prague, who had come with a large wardrobe of colored satin capes to be changed according to the liturgical calendar. I also had a tiny alligator, a real one, though stuffed, that a great-uncle had brought me from Florida. My alligator had a cloth skirt, a flowered straw hat, and a tiny suitcase. Mom insisted that Mrs. Alligator be on a separate shelf from Jesus to avoid any appearance of sacrilege. Even though I knew live alligators didn't dress, I longed to go to Florida myself one day—to that magical place of orange groves and palm trees—and have a firsthand look.

My bedroom alcove had the back window, but my sister's, where her matching bed paralleled mine, had the doors. Along her front wall, the door to the porch and the cellar door stood side by side. My sister had a matching bookcase complete with Mr. Alligator and a lot of toys. Sometimes at night just before we went to sleep, we'd toss a few tiny toys up through the latticework at the top of the room divider onto each other's beds. It was a game we enjoyed and one that wore thin on my parents rather quickly.

Dad had thoughtfully included a hall in his remodeling so we had some privacy, but the lack of doors on our dividers gave our rooms a sense of being on display that made our mother vigilant about keeping them in order. We'd been learning about Mendel in school at the time of construction, and so I dubbed our rooms our cells.

I was glad mine didn't have the cellar door. Who knew what might be in the basement at night? Daytime, of course, was another story. By day, our basement was a favored place to play.

When we'd moved to Cracker Hill from the Brooklyn section of Waterbury, the cellar had been a shadowy place with a dirt floor and fieldstone walls. At the heart of it stood its furnace, an asbestos-wrapped monster that looked like a headless snowman. At the back end, underneath the kitchen annex, was the subcellar, its low opening yawning like the entrance to a mineshaft.

My father changed all that, working nights to cement the floor and walls and to paint the furnace a cheerful red. His workbench next to the bulkhead door had pegboard for the hanging tools, all outlined in paint so that the saws and hammer could go back in their own places when he was through with them. Jar lids were nailed to the bottoms of the wall cabinets to hold the glass containers of assorted screws and nails, and the large vise mounted at one end was painted the same red as the furnace.

Probably other homes had the same workbench arrangement, but surely, we were the only house with murals on our cellar walls. Above the workbench, Snow White danced with the seven dwarfs. Another wall showed Bambi and Thumper next to Chip and Dale, who chattered across from a turbaned sultan mounted on an elephant, a little to the left of Donald Duck and his three nephews. Dad liked to sketch free hand on the walls, drawing inspiration from my comic books, and using paint left over from various household projects.

There were twin soapstone washtubs in the cellar, where my mother and grandmother did the weekly laundry with the help of a wringer washing machine. I liked to watch them feed the steaming wet clothes through the wringer to emerge from the other side flattened into unrecognizable shapes. When the wicker laundry baskets were full, we carried them up the stone cellar steps through the cellar's hatch doors and onto the back porch. Hung from the clothesline, they flapped in the breeze, magically restored to the everyday items I knew. In winter, the clothes froze and had to be gathered, boardlike, and arranged on the radiators to finish drying.

It's hard to believe, but my mother ironed everything, including Dad's socks and our towels. And when my mother's mother came to visit on weekdays, she'd iron too. On hot summer days, the ironing board was set up in the basement, the coolest spot in our house. When she was ready to plug in the iron, my mother called up the stairs to Grandma on the second floor to warn her. A fuse was sure to blow if the iron and the fan were on at the same time.

If a fuse did blow, one of us would put a penny in the fuse box behind the fuse. Because the fuse box was on the back wall by the subcellar's waist-high door, I worried that a hand would come out and grab me, so if it was my turn at the fuse box, I worked fast.

With or without someone ironing, the basement was a great place to play if you turned on all the lights. There was a flowered rug on the floor, my sister's toy bin, a few chairs, and my tin dollhouse from the Sears Roebuck catalogue. The house had a tiny battery-operated light inside. I never tired of rearranging the furniture and the tiny rubber animals that lived inside.

The rubber animals were not quite two inches high. They'd come from Woolworth's counter in packets of three, wrapped in cellophane. They may have been intended as pencil-top erasers for some people, but not for us. We named them and played with them until they were much the worse for wear. There was a poodle, a lion, and a panda in one packet, a monkey with a red derby in the other, keeping company with a teddy bear and an enchantingly pink elephant. Planning their adventures kept us busy all day, and I imagined that if I'd had the nerve to open the cellar door late at night, I'd have seen the little light burning in the dollhouse window as the rubber animals tended to their own business after hours.

Underneath the cellar steps, a rickety dining-room sideboard held albums of greeting cards my mother had saved. There were all the birthday wishes and Christmas cards and Valentines my father had sent her from the time they'd met as well as some recent ones waiting to be glued in.

"To My Sweetheart," read my favorite, an oversized red one with a padded white satin heart set in gold filigree. I knew Dad had sent that particular one from Newport, Rhode Island, during World War II. I'd seen photographs of him in his sailor's uniform, a slender dark-haired man of twenty. My father had enlisted in the navy, despite the fact that he hated water and had never learned to swim. Luckily, he'd been captain of the Leavenworth High School Rifle Team. And so, instead of putting out to sea, Dad spent the war years at the Newport Naval Base as a gunnery instructor. I wondered why he hadn't stayed in the navy. It looked like a lot more adventure than his postwar job of cable splicer at the Southern New England Telephone Company. But it remained yet another unsolved mystery, one my parents answered by saying,

"You're too young to understand."

Perhaps it had to do with security, because the men in my family took one job and kept it forever. Dad's father worked for a utility too, the Connecticut Light & Power Company. My mother's father worked for the City of Waterbury, in the park department. That was a place where it seemed you could stay on even past retirement. The case in point was the house at Hamilton Park, where the Park foreman was entitled to live. Although he had the job, Grandpa did not have the house. The previous foreman was allowed to remain there. At last, Grandpa took the job as Washington Park foreman because its four-room railroad flat in the park house was empty.

My dad and his father worked hard, so it seems amazing that they had the energy to put in extra hours at night on home improvements, never mind the school projects Dad helped me to make in the cellar on his workbench. Our standouts were a wooden ship with life rails rigged with string and tiny nails, a miniature altar for religion class fashioned from a cigar box painted silver, and a pinhole camera made from a coffee can.

Although the basement had its attractions, in better weather we bypassed it for our yard. My sister and I were partial to our swings made by Dad from pipes and painted silver. We liked to lean back, pumping hard for a soaring ride that put our feet nearly level with the top of the lilac bush. With our heads hanging upside down, we could imagine the sky as the deep blue sea. Clouds were islands shrouded in white mist, the leafy trees, distant continents. An occasional bird flying past became a fish of a rare species. The swings were a satisfying trip out of Waterbury on a slow afternoon.

Our swings were also excellent vantage points from which to observe our neighbors and their fascinating goings-on. Near us lived a glamorous young married couple with a little baby. The husband fenced and often after supper could be seen going off to a meet in his white fencing suit, carrying his foil.

A lot of walking went on at Cracker Hill, up and down Willow Street. It was "shank's mare," as Grandpa put it, for going to Mass or confession, to the markets and drugstores at the corners of the blocks, and sometimes just for an evening stroll and a visit. When we sat out on the front porch in the evenings, neighbors would stop for a chat as they went about their business. If a group of people passed, Grandpa's comment might be that they were straggling like "Brown's cows," an allusion to a long-gone farm on the west side of town somewhere near the site of municipal stadium.

It seemed that everyone had something remarkable about them. At one house where I'd gone to a birthday party, the parents had a giant rosary made out of horse chestnuts. It hung on the wall above their bed. A man on the next street made fishing lures as a hobby. I'd gone to his garage with my father to watch Dad paint an Indian chief in a multicolored feathered warbonnet on the man's canoe.

I'd met some of the kids my age when I'd made my First Holy Communion, and the dreams they'd shared when the nun asked us what we'd like to be when we grew up were impressive: a ballerina and a barrel racer, a jockey, the president. I was glad the nun hadn't asked me. My main idea was to go out west and be a cowgirl. I liked the idea of jazzy Western clothes and boots like Dale Evans wore. My fallback plan was to be a writer though I had no idea of what kind of stories I might tell.

Meanwhile, the neighbors' sagas went on around us. One afternoon, I overheard my mother telling my grandmother about a local scandal. It seemed someone's husband had come home from work early only to find his landlord in his bed. I knew where these people lived, and the story made sense to me. I imagined the landlord had gotten tired walking up to the top floor to collect his rent and had decided to nap.

Far more remarkable in my eyes was the daily routine of an elderly lady whom my grandmother said was an "old maid." Old Maid was a card game I played that had to do with matching pairs of cards. Whoever drew the card with the witch on it was stuck because there was no match for her in the deck. It seemed that "old maid" was synonymous with "witch." I felt certain that I did not want to be an old maid when I grew up, and yet there was something attractive about a lifestyle that included magic powers.

I always said hello to that neighbor when she passed by our house, and gradually we became friends. In the year before I started kindergarten, she sometimes invited me to visit. It was said that no one in the neighborhood had ever seen inside her house. Even the distant relatives who occasionally dropped by to check up on her were made to sit out on the back porch. We'd seen them, even in December, huddled there in their coats, their breath making frosty puffs against the winter sky.

One summer afternoon, my neighbor left her back door open when she went in to fetch a glass of water. I saw peeling salmon-colored wallpaper. On it, soiled white swans glided past dark lily pads. On the floor were stacks of old newspapers and bundles of clothes that reached to the top of the beadboard wainscoting. What seemed like a jungle of plants grew out of old coffee cans, and the yellowed lace curtains filtered the sun into swirling patterns on the cracked linoleum floor.

"So what was it like in there?" my mother and grandmother asked. The interior of our neighbor's house was a favorite neighborhood topic. We'd guessed at everything from priceless antiques to a mysterious hidden tunnel to Fort Knox. But I had no words to describe the glimpse I'd had of another way of living, or the feeling I'd gotten of time standing still inside my neighbor's house.

"I don't know," I replied. "I don't know."

Waterbury itself was home to exotic people, living legends my parents talked about such as Chief Two Moon and his magic elixir factory on East Main Street, and the city's own Mad Bomber, who'd made treks to New York to blow up Gotham City a little at a time.

I could see that I lived in a place with great scope for the imagination, as the heroine of *Anne of Green Gables* said of her island home.

Visitors to our house were almost always family. The neighbors usually visited by chatting across back fences or from front porches with each other, walking by. So when our doorbell rang during the daytime, it probably was a door-to-door salesman or a Jehovah Witness offering us copies of their magazines. For Witnesses, my mother simply said, "We don't want any. We're Catholic."

For salesmen, my mother said no from behind a closed door. It's a mystery to me how a salesman came to be in our kitchen one afternoon. Perhaps my grandmother had let him in out of curiosity because what he was selling was the latest thing: unbreakable dishes.

"Watch this," he said, throwing a five-piece table setting of hard plastic onto our kitchen floor. It was the floor Dad had washed and waxed only the night before.

"It takes any abuse," he continued and jumped on the meat platter, which slid a little toward us. The salesman mistook my mother's wide eyes expression for interest and offered her a special price if she bought today. My mother had a look, which Dad called "The Look." It meant "beware" when the right eyebrow went up and the left eyebrow went down. Mom's blue eyes glinted steel, and her mouth was an unsmiling straight line. I knew he was in trouble. Within seconds, the salesman and his sample case were on the other side of the door, his offers of an even better price to no avail.

The family company we had on the first floor was most often my mother's parents or her brother with my aunt and cousins. On the other hand, my grandparents on the second floor had a steady stream of guests. There were women Grandma called her lady friends, including one tiny woman with brightly rouged cheeks with whom she'd work at a silk mill in Watertown when they were girls. In addition, there was Grandma's large family of brothers and sisters.

They lived in places with names out of fairy tales, like Golden Hill and Pearl Lake Road, and the stories they told over cake and coffee in Grandma's kitchen kept me hanging on every word. There were cousins who played the accordion or tap danced in sequined costumes in dance recitals, adults who raised chinchillas for profit, great uncles who traveled to Florida and had seen alligators, great aunts who wore copper bracelets to ward off arthritis and who shut their poinsettias in dark closets to force them to bloom. Their anecdotes glowed with drama.

But often, when Grandma had company, my mother would order, "Stay downstairs where you belong."

It was her opinion that her side of the family, the Irish side, was superior because they were purebred. That meant they were all Irish, from Ireland itself, all the way back to when time began. Dad's side were French and Irish and Scotch, a mixed heritage my mother contrasted with her side as mongrels. Dad laughed off the canine analogy. He didn't mind being a mongrel. But I felt offended. How could I be judged and found lacking by the choice my mother herself had made in selecting my other parent? In an attempt to make the best of it, I coached my little sister in the finer points of walking on all fours and barking until Mom told us to knock it off.

If upstairs was off-limits for the evening, my sister and I took up our stations on the bottom step in the front hall where we could at least be close to the action. One cousin, the musician, had joined the navy, and the sight of him in his uniform the night he came to play for Grandma was breathtaking. Up the stairs he went with his mother of pearl-trimmed black accordion to play "Lady of Spain." We thought he looked as glamorous as Elvis and a whole lot more accessible.

I practiced swooning while the concert went on. It was something I'd seen on TV in an old movie where Judy Garland sang a love song to a photograph. I copied her, clasping my hands and shutting my eyes halfway.

"Are you okay?" Grandma called from the top of the stairs. I guessed she hadn't seen the same movie that I had.

My cousin's sister was beautiful, with curly black hair and big brown eyes. People described her as "petite" and "cute" and "vivacious." About me, they said, "quiet" and "reads a lot." I wished I could be like her, so confident in her circle skirts and matching sweater sets. But in my blue serge uniform jumper and brown oxfords, I was light-years away from being a teenager, and I knew it.

One afternoon after high school, she stopped by to give me a book.

"I got this for my birthday," she told me, "but it's more you than me." I was sitting in Grandma's kitchen rocker petting our cat. The book was *Little Women*, and my cousin was right. I read it five times that year, beginning it as soon as she'd left. As I read it, sitting by the window that looked out into our lilac tree, I peeled a tangerine. And so my first meeting with Marmee and her girls was bound in my memory with the smell of oranges in a Waterbury kitchen.

It was one of Grandma's brothers who brought the first lobsters I'd ever seen to our house. He hurried to her kitchen with a large damp brown paper bag from which a dark greenish claw bound with a red elastic band protruded. Grandma was waiting, water boiling in the blue enamel pot she used for corn on the cob.

My great uncle upended the bag, setting the lobsters loose on the kitchen linoleum where they scrabbled about, waving their claws. When they were lowered into the pot, I closed my eyes and put my hands over my ears, expecting to hear them scream like Joan of Arc. But all there was was the bubble and hiss of the water as they turned from green to red.

Another of Grandma's brothers lived in the country and had started a chinchilla farm in his basement. It was a happy surprise when he brought one of them to us as an Easter present. My mother shuddered at its resemblance to a rat and banished it from our house. Grandma allowed it to live upstairs in a corner of her kitchen in its little wire cage. We never named our pet despite our fondness for holding it and watching our hands disappear into its deep, soft coat when we petted it. Even grown-up, our chinchilla wasn't that big. It would have taken a million of him to make a coat.

Eventually my great uncle gave up on his idea of a ranch. He told us how he opened the cages lined up in tiers in his garage and released the animals into the woods around his house. Sometimes, late at night as I lay in bed, I'd picture the chinchillas dancing in the moonlight like the animals in my sister's picture book *The Rabbits' Wedding*.

Of all the visitors who rang our bell on Willow Street, the strangest situation arrived one day in a G. Fox and Company delivery van. Grandma had ordered bedspreads from the store in Hartford, and when she answered the door to sign for her package, she recognized the deliveryman. He was her long-lost half brother. They hadn't seen each other in over thirty years.

Grandma and her brother embraced in the front hall and called to us to come in for an introduction. Then they went upstairs to catch up on family news.

No one else got a delivery from that G. Fox truck that day. Grandma's brother stayed till Grandpa came home from work, and they'd all had dinner. When he left, they kissed and said a tearful good-bye.

My grandmother spent the rest of the evening on the phone calling her other siblings to tell them whom she'd seen. Everyone agreed that it was an amazing coincidence he'd come to our door in the first place. But the most amazing part to me was that after that day, we never saw or heard from him again.

Our Family

I never thought to ask, when I was growing up on Cracker Hill, how so many different nationalities had come to live in Waterbury. If I had asked, I'd have learned that they'd come for the jobs. And the bottom line for that was brass. Although at first, the city workers were Yankees, it wasn't long before waves of immigrants arrived from Canada and Europe.

Even in the fifties, Waterbury was far from the melting pot analogy my history book used to describe America. The city seemed more like a stew, where all the ingredients remained separate, but somehow cooperated for a tasty final product. Italians lived in the North End or Town Plot. The French were in the South End. Irish were in the Abrigador or Out East. The Brooklyn section of town was Lithuanian. These lines blurred as people moved about, but the big picture still had continuity.

What all the different parts of town had in common was a strong sense of community, held together by ties of language and custom, which often showed most in the various festivals of each group's churches. Who could forget Our Lady of Mount Carmel's annual procession or St. Anne's Mass in French?

My own neighborhood was the world brought down to size, a place where nationalities mixed and intermarried as a matter of course. It was a rich diversity. But unlike other parts of town where neighbors seemed rooted, Willow Street was filled with families who stayed awhile and then moved on.

My own family was a mix of nationalities who had come, just like the people in my history book, to find work. No doubt that the things they experienced were much like the adventures of other Waterburians. But as a child, I found my family unique, and their history as wonderful as any book on the shelves at the Silas Bronson Library. I never tired of asking to hear their stories one more time.

Dad's mother had a Scotch Yankee father and a French Canadian mother. The family had migrated south through New England's mill towns to Waterbury following work. Grandma had been put to work early, as had Dad's father.

Neither one had had the chance to finish grammar school. Dad's parents met when Grandma was fifteen, boarding out to work at Hemingway's silk mill in Watertown. She glossed over what factory work had been like, preferring to talk about the good times.

"Saturday nights, I'd play the piano in the rooming-house parlor. All of us girls would sing. Your grandfather came to town to court another girl, but I got him away from her. 'May you never have a day's luck in your life,' she told me." Here Grandma would laugh, indicating the lucky life she felt she'd had in spite of her ex-friend's curse.

When the first of her three children was born, Grandpa was in France for the Great War. I'd seen his name on a bronze plaque attached to a monumental rock on a grassy island in Watertown, dedicated to the men who'd served as soldiers. My grandfather refused ever to talk about the war or the battle of Chateau-Thierry and Belleau Woods—where he'd been shot, gassed, and left for dead. He kept his medals tucked away out of sight, preferring to forget or trying to. But summers, swimming at Lake Quassapaug, the deep scars peppering both his legs from the bullet holes were a reminder to us all.

Dad's father's parents were a mix of nationalities: an Irish grandmother, a French Canadian grandfather. It was that great-grandfather, a carpenter, who'd built the monolithic three-family house at 619 Riverside Street on the banks of the Naugatuck River. Grandpa had grown up there along with three sisters and a brother, and most of them still lived in the house across from the Riverside Cemetery long after we'd moved to Cracker Hill. On our Sunday visits, we'd sometimes cross the street to visit Grandma's old landlady at the corner of Riverside and Summit Street, though my parents never cared to return to their old rent on Washington Avenue. Dad's parents sometimes talked over my head in a rapid slangy French that made me wish I was bilingual. We were an ethnic exception that proved the rule of what nationalities lived where in the city, since the Brooklyn section was predominantly Lithuanian.

Mom's parents were from Killarney, in County Kerry. They'd been in Ireland since time began, according to my grandfather, who loved a good story. His tales ran to adventures of fighting with the Black and Tans or hunting leprechauns with his little dog, questing for their elusive pot of gold. Grandma's reminiscences were more wistful, recalling her life as a girl.

Her house in Killarney was called Dinis cottage, and it was on the Middle Lake. Tourists boating through the lakes to admire the views stopped at Dinis for tea, and Grandma's family provided it. Her descriptions of dolls and dressmakers sounded wonderful, and I was curious about how she'd been able to leave it all behind. Grandpa's family still lived nearby where they worked on the local estate, the Muckross House, where Grandpa had been a gardener.

Perhaps they'd planned to stay in Ireland, but Grandma's father would not hear of either of his two daughters leaving home.

And so my grandparents eloped. I loved to hear Grandpa tell how Grandma's father had followed them to the railroad station in his horse and carriage in an attempt to stop their plan. They'd eluded capture and made their way to Wales, where Grandpa had found work in a coal mine with his brother Pat. Burry Port, Wales, was where my mother was born, in a tiny row house on the second floor.

It was easy to see how glad they'd been to reach America. Grandpa's uncle in Waterbury guaranteed him a place to stay and a job at Scovill's mills, so they bypassed Ellis Island. But Grandpa, true to form, gave the story a twist. When the family drove to New York to meet the boat, Grandpa stepped off with not only a wife but an eighteen-month-old baby as well, so when they returned to 166 Walnut Street, there was a scramble to find a place for everyone to sleep.

All the family on Mom's side in Waterbury belonged to Grandpa. Grandma's family was known to me only by the letters that arrived from her sister Lizzie. These were pale blue envelopes marked Par Avion that folded open like origami, fragile missives written in a shaky backhand script.

"We are all well here, T.G.," they usually began, "T.G." being the abbreviation for "thank God." On Saint Patrick's Day, our annual packet of real shamrocks made their way across the ocean to us, and at Christmas came a holy greeting card. It was all I knew of them except for the cousin who'd written once to say that if I ever got to Ireland, she'd give me a ride on a donkey.

My own parents had been high school sweethearts, and their gold and onyx Leavenworth High School rings nestled side by side in the ring tray of Mom's red-lined jewelry box. Dad had graduated in 1941, just in time to enlist in the navy for World War II. He and my mother married secretly. Her father would have said she was too young.

I arrived at the end of the war in 1945, at Thanksgiving time. My parents told each other that the deep V mark on my forehead from the forceps delivery was symbolic of the *V* for "victory" that celebrated the war's end. My father had walked from Washington Avenue to St. Mary's in a snowstorm because the snow was too deep to take his car, a detail I found romantic and picturesque.

Born into a family of storytellers, I learned to add my own narratives shaped from what I'd seen and done each day when we sat down to supper together at night or on weekends when we met with the family for tea. All of my family's different stories made up the big picture of where we fit, on Cracker Hill and in Waterbury, our town.

Downtown

In the fifties, ladies dressed up to go downtown. It was a ritual with significance. Downtown was the hub of the city, and you never knew whose path might cross yours. The women in my family felt that it was vital to look one's best in public. And watching my grandmother prepare for her weekly event elevated grooming from routine to ritual.

The foundation of Grandma's preparation was her corset, a pale peach brocade affair custom made for her by the corset lady, who lived west of us at the corner of Waterville and Wyman Streets in a rambling Victorian house converted to apartments. The lady came to our house for the fittings of the garment, a washboard-ribbed band with boned stays like long metal wands that circled Grandma's midsection and stretched from the top of her rib cage to midhip.

"You'll get yours someday," Grandma confided as the corset lady laced her tight. I liked to pretend Grandma was donning armor like the stuff the knights in my *Ivanhoe* Classic Comic wore. But not even I could romanticize wearing such a contraption for real. Little ribbon streamers with garters at their ends dangled from the corset's lower level, waiting to be hooked onto Grandma's heavy support stockings that she wore for her varicose veins.

Over the top of the corset went her brassiere and over that, a full slip. Then it was comb-out time for the triple row of carefully coiled pin curls. Grandma's "good" clothes came next, from their garment bag next to the stalwart everyday cotton housedresses. In fall and spring, she often selected her navy blue suit with a lacy white blouse. In summer, a cooler choice was a cotton sundress, perhaps with a white piqué bolero jacket for modesty in public. And always, for dress up, there were high-heeled shoes.

"Can I pick out your hat?" I'd ask. Grandma had a collection. On the closet shelf were hatboxes with flowered hats like tiny gardens. Summer hats came from Jo-Belle's where they were arranged on wall shelves according to color.

Winter hats were more substantial creations of felt and feathers, winking with the occasional fake jewel. Those hats came from Oelkler's.

Drawing on her white gloves, she'd add a linen handkerchief to her pocketbook, check to see that her hem discreetly covered her slip. A dash of After Five perfume by Auvergne, a touch of Charles of the Ritz Pink Geranium lipstick, and she was down the front hall stairs and out the door.

Across Willow Street in front of Delaney's Drugstore was where we caught our bus, the one marked Reidville/Overlook. Seen from a distance, Grandma looked like someone I barely knew, formal and mysterious. And when she came home in the late afternoon, stepping off the bus just beyond Dave's Superette in time to start Grandpa's supper, I welcomed her as if she had been away in a foreign land for a long, long time.

"What's in the bags?" was the question of the hour, closely followed by "did you bring me anything?" The answer was always yes.

Grandma's taste ran to paper dolls, doll clothes, and books. Once the book was *Hiawatha*, a story with a giant sturgeon that I found alarming. A better present was the paper doll of Vera Ellen, a movie star who was said to have a sixteen-inch waist.

My mother's mother always arrived with presents too, but she leaned toward miniatures from Woolworth's where she caught the bus with her transfer from the other end of town. Her choice of little plastic baby carriages and cradles with tiny babies held firmly in place by elastic were equaled only by the real shells that opened when placed in water, revealing an elaborate paper flower. Those toys, though I didn't know it at the time, were both a postwar legacy and a taste of things to come, all of them marked Made In Japan.

Sometimes Grandma took me along with her when she went downtown. I dressed, too, for those occasions in patent leather shoes and my Sunday best. In winter, Grandma wore her gray coat with its collar of curly Persian lamb, and I, my coat with velvet buttons. I liked the dressy look and dreaded my daily school uniform, in particular the brown lace-up oxford shoes that looked to me like something a man would wear in prison in a foreign land.

Downtown at any time, I tried to steer my grown-up away from the Handy Kitchen, where teenagers hung out after school, eating french fries and sipping Cokes. My mother's mother was partial to the rice pudding at the Handy Kitchen, and if she'd met me at Notre Dame after school, it was a given that we'd be stopping in before we took the bus.

In my navy uniform with beanie hat and white gloves, I'd try to look invisible among the horde of high schoolers, whom I saw as the height of sophistication. I'd clutch the handle of my bulging leather bookbag monogrammed "B. J. S." on its side in gold as we maneuvered for a booth. We'd sit there for what seemed like a lifetime as Grandma savored her pudding and I gnawed at my soda straw wishing in vain that she preferred the Waldorf Cafeteria on the other side of the Green, a place where no teenager was ever seen to go.

Dad's mother liked to lunch when we went downtown, and our destination was always the Front Page Restaurant. It was on Exchange Place, just beyond Bauby's newsstand. Men congregated there, passing the time of day and occasionally, to Grandma's disgust, spitting on the sidewalk, so when we passed them, we moved smartly along, averting our eyes to discourage any attempt at conversation.

Entering the air-conditioned dimness of the Front Page on a bright afternoon, passing through the bar to the dining room, gave me an exotic feeling of raciness. I read the tall menu carefully although I always ended up ordering spaghetti. Heavy white linen napkins and a dish of butter pats on ice added to the illusion that the dark vinyl booth where we sat was on the Orient Express, speeding us to an unknown destination. After lunch, I'd collect a book of matches with the restaurant name, pocket a few pastel mints, and head up Bank Street with Grandma to the stores.

The Howland-Hughes department store was my favorite, simply because there was so much of it, on so many floors. It was like a city in itself. In its basement was a cafeteria where shoppers could take a brown plastic tray and select their own food. Red Jell-O with a blob of whipped cream on top and a little green tin pot of tea were my usual choices. I'd pour the tea carefully into the thick white china cup banded in brown. The cups themselves were smoothly glazed, but their rims were rough, probably from being stacked a multitude of times upside down. It was an odd sensation, sipping from them, but no one else seemed to mind.

Wherever I went in Waterbury, I had the uneasy feeling that someone was watching. It wasn't simply because of the nuns' warnings about heavenly observance. It was the real thing. My school stressed something called "deportment," which meant acting like a credit to Notre Dame Academy, especially when in uniform. If a girl was seen misbehaving in uniform, particularly downtown or on the bus home, someone nearly always called the school to report it. Our school was small, and it didn't take much in the way of detective work for our principal to figure out who'd done it. Next morning, the offender's head was sure to roll. Days when I was out of uniform, I was off duty, so to speak. But still, you never knew. And so I sat up straight and kept my elbows off the tabletop.

The cafeteria in Howland-Hughes was one of the basement's many attractions. The toy department was another. Directly across from the gray stone stairs down was the doll case. When walking down, I kept my eyes on the smooth wooden railing until I'd reached the bottom step, then lifted them fast to maximize the impact. The Madame Alexander dolls were front and center, sparkling in the overhead lights that picked up the gold of the fairy's magic wand, the ballerina's silver spangled tutu. Best of all was the bride doll, a vision in white satin, her blonde hair tastefully arranged beneath her tulle veil accented with white velvet rosebuds.

In the back corner by the elevator was a wooden phone booth with a glass door and a tiny seat, useful if you knew somebody to call. There was an operator in the elevator, a lady on a chair who asked what floor you wanted. We usually selected the third because that was where the ladies' room was, tucked behind the housewares and slipcover sections.

Beyond its heavy wooden door, the floor changed from the wood of the merchandise area to a pattern of small eight-sided black-and-white tiles in a geometric style. There were three sinks to cut down on waiting time, but the row of toilets had slots in their doors for nickels. The ladies in this room always cooperated with each other by holding the doors open.

"A nickel indeed," someone usually muttered to Grandma as she ushered me in.

Sitting down inside was out of the question until the entire rim of the black seat was ringed with the uncooperative slippery toilet paper squares.

"Never forget to do this," Grandma admonished. "Otherwise . . . ." She meant that public bathrooms were filled with other people's germs, horrible ones like the cartoons of tooth decay in television toothpaste commercials. Some of the girls at school hinted at things that were even worse though never specified. One thing I did feel sure of was that it was impossible to get a baby that way since the nuns had explained that children came only after the sacrament of marriage.

With our mission accomplished, we'd walk down the back staircase to lingerie and hats, then on to the main floor to see what was new in notions, costume jewelry, and handbags. High on the fourth floor next to the furniture department, ladies were having their hair done, but the fragrance of permanent wave lotion did not reach this far down. And so we were primed for sniffing all the perfumes on the counter by the front door. A quick spritz of whatever took our fancy on the sample tray, and we were off across Bank Street to Engelman's and Worth's.

Stores on this side of Bank Street were built into a hill. This meant that although you could enter under the watchful eye of the M. A. Green freestanding sidewalk clock shaped like a dark green metal lollipop, you could leave from another street entirely. The shortcut to South Main was particularly handy in rain or in snowy weather.

Worth's, the store with "smiling service," was where I got my haircut on the second floor near preteen dresses and the Girl Scout section. Here, the aroma of permanent wave lotion was strong. Grandma herself, applying the formula at home that turned her hair from straight to wavy, often explained that one had to suffer to be beautiful. To me it seemed a choice like the one in a song my mother sometimes sang, about being in between the devil and the deep blue sea. I hoped that someday I could be beautiful, but I definitely did not want to suffer for it.

One year, Worth's instituted a club for girls that met in the store on Saturday mornings. The club had its own diamond-shaped black pins that read "STT" in white letters. The initials decoded to mean "smaller than teens." We didn't do much more than to walk around with books on our heads to improve our posture, and to say thanks for the complimentary nail-care kits, but the weekly visits were an opportunity to see what was new in the second floor's display of Ginny dolls and accessories.

Ginny was my passion. She had the kind of stuff you'd dream of for yourself if you could imagine being the kind of girl who had a white rabbit fur coat and matching hat, resort wear, ski wear, monogrammed luggage, and an extensive set of pink bedroom furniture with your face on it—all for a doll only eight inches high.

Ginny had a baby sister in whom I had no interest whatsoever and a big sister, Jill, who was an inspiration to keep on going toward the teen years. Jill, her feet frozen into high-heel position, had bosoms and attitude. Her clothes ran to velvet toreador pants and strapless dresses, rhinestone-trimmed sunglasses, and lacy lingerie. A successful trip downtown for me meant a new outfit for one of them.

Mom's idea of shopping heaven was the sales at Windsor Curtain shop or Bedford's. Lincoln's and Washington's birthdays meant red-letter days for our beds and windows. I looked forward to the changes too. They added fresh perspective to familiar rooms in the same way that seeing classmates out of uniform on dress-up occasions gave routine classes on those days a new dimension.

Shopping with my grandmothers was best because they had time to linger, and downtown had so many things to savor. When it was time to head home, the bus we took could be caught either at the Green or in front of Woolworth's. My grandmothers usually voted for the Green because of its benches, where you could rest and watch the pigeons pecking along, looking for food beneath the slatted seats. People sometimes shared their snack from the Carmel Corn store with the pigeons.

Although I liked the shiny, oil-slick iridescence of the green and purple rings around the gray ones' necks, my favorite pigeons were the beige ones. They looked to me like the pictures of the Holy Ghost in my catechism book. Any one of those dignified birds strolling on little red feet might be him on a reconnaissance mission from the Immaculate Conception Church on the far side of the Green.

Seated on my park bench vantage point, I could look east toward the gray stone clock with four faces that did not keep equal time and see the Carrie Welton Fountain, where North Main and East Main intersected. Crowned with a statue of her favorite mount, the fountain had been a gift to Waterbury from Carrie Welton, wealthy explorer and lover of animals, for the comfort of horses.

Free-spirited saddleless knight shook his verdigris mane from on top of his stone pedestal high above the watering troughs, immortalized despite the fact that he'd kicked Carrie's father to death in the very stable where he'd drunk from a gold-rimmed dish with his name on it. These days, yellow cabs waited for fares beneath knight's raised right hoof.

At the opposite end of the Green across from Saint John's Episcopal Church and its rose window was a war memorial with statues on all four sides. A Civil War soldier and a lady in flowing robes kept an eye on the traffic cruising along Main Street. If they had looked far enough up East Main past the Lincoln Store and Curtis Art, they might have seen Mr. Peanut strolling along, shaking hands.

Mr. Peanut was a person dressed in a black leotard and a black top hat. His arms ended in white-gloved hands. His body was a huge peanut fashioned of an unidentifiable hard substance with little grooves to make it look authentic. Mr. Peanut wore a monocle on the head part of his shell over one eye. And through the cutouts in his costume, you could see his eyes and the occasional flick of his tongue through his mouth hole.

You either liked Mr. Peanut or you didn't. Grown-ups smiled and took the pennies off cards he handed out for the peanut store. Little children were often terrified and hid behind their mothers. Mr. Peanut was okay with me because I liked his wares, but I still preferred to see him at a distance, at least from the other side of the street.

If we had opted to take the bus home from Woolworth's instead, a good idea if it was cold outside or raining, we'd go inside to have a look around. I liked to start at the back of the store, where cages of ice blue and lime green parakeets fluttered from perch to perch in their cages, pulling themselves along the bars with their little beaks and claws, chirping to each other.

Schools of goldfish swam in tanks past stacks of little round bowls, their future homes. If you wanted to give your fish a taste of adventure, you could add a tiny castle, a mermaid, or a wrecked galleon to the bottom of their bowl. There was even a miniature treasure chest with plastic jewels being opened by a deep-sea diver in a heavy costume straight out of Jules Verne's *Twenty Thousand Leagues Under the Sea*, another story I'd read in Classic Comic form. As to the turtles, my own had come from this very store, and I felt no need to linger watching them scramble around on top of each other, jockeying for a tenuous position on top.

Midway down one side of Woolworth's was the lunch counter. Its back wall was tiled in beige, with a bas-relief cornucopia of fruits in red and blue. You could sit and swivel in a brown leatherette seat with a black metal back while a uniformed waitress prepared your deep-dish apple pie, a specialty of the house.

"Coke! The pause that refreshes!" read one sign. If you agreed and ordered one, the waitress prepared it by squirting the dark syrup into a glass, then adding soda water. The Coke-logoed glass arrived beaded with moisture, its paper-wrapped straw stuck to its damp side. If there was time after we'd been refreshed, we'd stop by the ribbon counter, where Grandma bought my hair bows by the yard, in the years when I had long curls.

Lined up side by side on spools, the ribbons shimmered enticingly. It was impossible to say which ones I liked best. The plaid taffeta ones were jaunty, but the watered silk ribbons with pink or yellow roses down their centers were as appealing as the flowers I'd seen in illustrations of *The Secret Garden*, a book our teacher read to us in school, some afternoons, as we waited at our desks for dismissal.

Sometimes when we got off the bus at Willow and Ridgewood, we'd find that we'd left our umbrella behind, hooked over the glass separator of one of the wooden counters at Woolworth's, perhaps the candy counter. The amazing thing was that when one of us went back for it, the lost umbrella was always just where we'd left it, waiting for us.

Beyond Woolworth's heading up East Main were the movie theaters. A few doors beyond W. T. Grant and the White Tower, a white porcelain-sided grille that was known for its square hamburgers, was the State. It was the newer of the two theaters downtown, with red carpets and a brass and glass popcorn stand.

The State Theater was where Rosalind Russell had appeared for the world premier of her movie, *Girl Rush* in August of 1955. Rosalind was a native Waterburian, and I passed her old home each day as I went back and forth to school. It was an impressive Victorian house, suited to the funeral parlor it had become. My school was taught by the same order of nuns who had taught Rosalind, the Congregation of Notre Dame, from Montreal, Canada. Those nuns taught at Waterbury Catholic High as well as Notre Dame, and it was with regularity that we heard how Rosalind, even from the wilds of the West Coast and Hollywood, kept in touch with her favorite teachers to let them know she had not wavered from her morals and had kept her Catholic faith.

Whoever booked the movies at the State had faith too. All the religious epics seemed to play there, including *The Robe*, the *Ten Commandments*, and *Ben-Hur*. *Ben-Hur* made a lasting impression on me, not for the famous chariot race scenes, but for the gruesome affliction of the lepers. For months afterward, I prayed each night not to contract leprosy and checked my skin fearfully after every bath.

The most memorable of all movies at the State was seen in the company of my schoolmates. It was the story of Maria Goretti, a young Italian girl up for sainthood in the Catholic Church. The nuns lined us up in pairs, and we walked from Church Street up East Main to the movies. All of the sixth, seventh, and eighth graders in our blue serge jumpers, blue beanies, white gloves, and brown oxford shoes marched into the State to watch the beautiful Blessed Maria refuse to do something with a wild-eyed dark-haired young man who stabbed her repeatedly and violently to death for that refusal.

"What did he want her to do, anyway?" was the question most of us asked each other. For sure, she'd refused to kiss him, but that hardly seemed enough to have provoked such a reaction on his part. Some of the older girls whispered knowingly to each other but refused to share what they knew with us. And so we asked our nun.

"Maria chose to keep her body a pure temple of the Holy Ghost," was her enigmatic reply. "Pray for the grace to do the same yourself."

Being a temple struck me as a tall order, particularly since I had no idea of what might be involved. At least with leprosy I knew what to watch out for. But as to Maria Goretti's situation, I was clueless, except for the uneasy new thought that dark-haired men could prove dangerous.

Across from the State was Waterbury's other downtown movie theater. Its official name was Loew's Poli Palace, but we called it simply the Palace. It had a sweeping double staircase of white marble and deep purple velvet draperies. Mirrors covered the lobby walls all the way to the ceiling, where three crystal chandeliers hung in a row.

If you looked closely, you'd see that the marble staircase was really fabricated to look like marble, and that the drapes were faded and musty. But no one went to the movies to find fault, and from a distance, the effect was regal, like being inside a castle. The Palace was the perfect setting for movies like Disney's *Cinderella* and *Sleeping Beauty*. And afterward, if you'd sat in the balcony and worn a dress, you could sweep down those almost-marble stairs and watch yourself do so in the cloudy mirrors framing the center hall.

A block farther east of the theaters was Crosby High School, a yellow brick building on a corner of a busy intersection. In the middle of the intersection stood a yellow brick tower, a bit like the pulpit our parish priest climbed each Sunday to deliver his sermon at Mass. The traffic tower was manned by a policeman with a whistle and white gloves, busily directing the snarl of busses, cars, and trucks.

Our nuns had schooled us never to say "cop," a term they deemed vulgar and disrespectful. But just as telling someone not to think of a purple cow guarantees they'll think of nothing else, their admonitions produced a similar effect in me. Sometimes the cop on duty in the tower found himself facing a car gone haywire. The officer would be shaken in his perch by the crash though the seemingly indestructible tower would remain standing.

My Irish grandfather had a take on the situation that he enjoyed acting out for us over tea. His contention was that if the crash car was a jalopy, the officer would hang on tight. But if it was a Cadillac, he'd jump from the tower and yell, "I'm hit!" to collect the insurance money. Since we had a policeman in the family through marriage, this may have explained why Grandpa was not everyone's favorite.

Like most of his stories, the glass slippers like Cinderella's he meant to find for me or the pony he might bring to live in our backyard on Willow, Grandpa's tower tale was purely a flight of fancy. But the sight of him rolling on the living-room rug acting out his story while Grandma hovered overhead threatening to smack him with the flyswatter gave an extra zip to our Sunday visits. And when we drove along East Main Street, we could never keep from grinning when we waved to the policeman on duty above us in his pillar of yellow brick.

One street in Waterbury that lived up to its name was Grand Street. The gray stone post office was there, its bas-relief panels showing the history of communication from the first messenger to the pony express, through ships and trains to planes. The first and last of the eleven panels showed the world suspended in space, a big round ball with wavy-sided North and South Americas. My favorite panel showed a tiny single engine propeller plane flying toward a rising sun. The only thing that could have made the illustration more complete for someone like me who was raised on TV Western shows like *Lone Ranger* and *Hopalong Cassidy*, would have been the addition of a few Indians sending smoke signals from the top of a butte while a wagon train rolled along below.

Grand Street also was home to Waterbury's city hall. Designed by Cass Gilbert, it had a wide white marble piazza with twin flagpoles and gigantic twin urns. In the center of the piazza was a two-tiered marble fountain with a wide, shallow base that seemed to encourage thoughts of wading on hot summer afternoons. The second floor of the city hall was in brick, and its roof was crowned with a golden dome. Inside, the building was all marble.

In one corner of the lobby near the stairs was a concession stand run by a blind man. People asked for candy or cigarettes, and he obliged, moving deftly behind the counter, putting his hands on the very thing requested, and making change without hesitation. How he did it, I could not imagine. I'd tried it at home myself, eyes closed, and found it impossible to tell a Snickers from a Milky Way, a quarter from a fifty-cent piece.

If you walked up the stairs to the landing, you could look down into the interior courtyard with its benches and rosebushes.

One wall of the enclosed garden was formed by the jail and police station attached to city hall on the library side of the building. I knew that men were often locked inside the jail cells behind barred windows though I never saw anyone from my city hall vantage point. My Girl Scout troop had had a tour once, gawking at an empty cell with a metal cot.

"You girls don't need to worry," the officer on duty had told us. "You'll never end up here."

In my family, perhaps because so many police and firemen were Irish, we held them in great esteem for the work they did protecting us, and I took his word as gospel. How nice it was at this end of Grand Street next to Library Park and its benches shaded by leafy trees. It was all so orderly and safe that I felt sure any crimes committed in town were small ones.

The downtown firehouse was also housed in city hall behind another of the inner courtyard's walls. It was a more welcoming sight than the jail, its doors open in good weather to show the big hook and ladder trucks shined up and ready to roll. These doors opened onto Field Street and were next to the armory's brick fortress. Across the street, one block over on Cottage Place was the Boys' Club, and on the corner of Cottage and Bank Street, the enormous Buckingham Building, another citadel-like structure that anchored Grand Street.

Across from city hall was the Chase building, designed by Cass Gilbert for the Chase Brass Company as a fraternal twin to compliment Waterbury's municipal headquarters. Its front courtyard and facade with high-arched windows were done in gray stone, and though I'd never been inside, I imagined it was just as impressive in its interior as city hall.

Chase was Chase Brass and Copper, the same industry that had produced the American Brass headquarters on Grand Street across from the train station. That building curved to follow the street as it swept along Meadow Street to Grand. American Brass had heavy brass doors that were polished regularly. At each corner of the front doors was a strange creature, half-man and half-scrolled pedestal, fashioned out of the golden metal. The figures grinned behind their pointy beards at passersby, the company's armless sentinels.

So many people passed by each day, many of them on their way to or from the train station. The station was huge, built on a scale comparable to its looming clock tower high above the tops of the elms and maples. The tower was visible from nearly every spot in town, and the movement that ran clocks on each of its four sides was made in the city by the Waterbury Clock Company.

Inside the station was cool and dim with high ceilings and long wooden benches. Footsteps echoed on the terrazzo floors, and the grand scale of the waiting room seemed designed to remind travelers of what a big world it was into which they were going. By the time Grandma and I went from Waterbury to Hartford on my first trip by train, the Waterbury *Republican-American* newspaper had begun its takeover of the building, and the Knights of Columbus had erected a memorial to Father McGivney, their founder, facing away from the newspaper office toward Grand Street. Father was a Waterbury native from the Brooklyn section of town, and it was said by some that his statue turned its back on the newspaper building because the mayor, a knight himself, had differences of opinion from the paper's owner.

On occasions when we took the train, we went to a brass-barred window to buy our tickets from a man with a visor on his head. With the tickets tucked safely in Grandma's purse, we waited on the platform by the baggage cart to begin our trip. Grandma's main purpose was to visit her brother in Hartford. Mine was to visit G. Fox and its stellar toy department.

Carrying my own small suitcase on board the silver-sided train seemed incredibly glamorous, probably because I'd seen so many movies involving train rides on our television's *"Early Show."* The porter handed me up the steps, and the conductor called, "All aboard," and the piercing whistle of the train as we left the station and swayed along the track staggering to our seats convinced me that a train ride was the ultimate way to go.

Not all travelers in and out of Waterbury took the train. Quite a few of them used the Greyhound bus. Its terminal was downtown on the Green near the Lincoln Store. Grandma's brother who lived in a neighboring state arrived by bus for his annual visit. I knew when he was coming because Grandma would appear downstairs in our kitchen to remind Dad to pick him up.

"Oh, Ma," he'd moan. "What if someone sees me? At least get him to arrive at night. Late. When it's dark out."

I found that great-uncle fascinating and could not understand my father's dismay. Tall and thin, with suits cut in the Western fashion with yoked jackets, my uncle favored garments of pale blue or green, string ties that fastened with holders shaped like little cow heads, and best of all, a cowboy hat.

Grandma's brother had once appeared on the Ted Mack *Original Amateur Hour*. His talent was that he played a one-man band. Ted Mack's contestants were rated by the applause meter in his studio, and even though it couldn't hear me, I'd clapped loud and long for my famous relative.

"Can I get a harmonica?" I'd asked after we'd turned off our black-and-white Philco TV. I figured I already had a head start on show business since I had the cowboy hat that had come with my six-shooter cap pistols.

"Over my dead body," Dad replied. "I knew it was a mistake to let you watch."

Having ruled out television appearances, I next fixed my sights on the Knights of Columbus where my best friend's father was a knight. They'd taken me along the day the Waterbury Chapter marched up Grand Street to dedicate Father McGivney's bronze statue. I was wowed by their purple-lined capes and their huge black hats with long white curling plumes like the one Captain Hook wore in *Peter Pan*. After the speeches beneath the statue's raised right arm, we all went back to the clubhouse on Dube Lane. The men spoke to each other like brothers, and their camaraderie made me think my dad might like to join their club. I liked the idea of my father with a sword and myself the daughter of a knight. But when I suggested it, he said no. I could not believe he could pass up the opportunity for a touch of grandeur.

"Look," he said. "If I ever get the urge to dress up and run around town, I'll at least wait till Halloween and get some candy for it." And with that, he went out to wax the car. I was disappointed, but my mother explained to me that some men are joiners, and some are not. I consoled myself with the thought that I at least had my friend's father to admire on occasions when the knights dressed formally for their regal events.

Father McGivney's statue kept company with one of Benjamin Franklin in front of the Silas Bronson Library. But unlike the saintly priest who stood, Ben sat on his own sculpted bench. Day in and day out, he leaned on his cane, feet comfortably apart, and watched the people pass the library. Some Waterburians thought that the statue was of Silas Bronson himself. But they were the ones who hadn't acquainted themselves with the porte-cochered, ivy-wrapped brownstone building and its staff of lady librarians.

The library looked like a mansion with its main entrance to one side. Broad steps led up to the massive oak doors underneath the overhanging roof where a carriage might have drawn up to discharge its passengers in inclement weather. The library had high ceilings and oak floors to match the paneling on its walls. Above the fireplace mantle was an oil portrait of Silas Bronson. Beneath it, glimmering beneath a fine coating of dust, a brass plaque told the story of his bequest to Waterbury.

Footsteps echoed loudly in the quiet hall where the librarians sat behind their low, wide counter keeping an eye on all who entered.

"The children's room is that way, dear," they'd tell me, pointing toward the carved oak staircase that led to the second floor, the place where I'd gotten my first library card. How excited I'd been when I understood that I could borrow all the books I wanted, six at a time, from their well-stocked shelves. But that was then. Now the books I wanted were elsewhere, on the first floor.

To pause, seeming to study the plaque, then to glide quickly toward the stair and past it through a narrow door that led to the annex was a plan I carried out as often as I could with determination and a pounding heart. There were no librarians in the annex. There was nothing but books. They covered all four walls of the long, narrow brick addition from floor to ceiling. At right angles to the walls were more rows of shelves with thousands more books, stacked higher than I could reach by standing on my toes and reaching out my hand.

Beneath the casement windows were window seats framed by the ivy on the outside walls that rustled in summer in the slightest breeze. On sunny days, little motes of dust hung suspended in the shafts of light that filtered through the deep-set windows. It was so quiet in the annex that even the sound of a turning page sounded loud. Here I could take down any book I chose and read it uninterrupted. At home, my perpetual reading disturbed my mother.

"You can't have your nose in a book all the time," she'd say. "Go outside. Take a walk. Do something." But what I wanted most was to read and to be, for the time I read, outside myself and in someone else's life.

I began my reading in the annex in the *W* section, because it was within easy reach on the low shelves and close to a window seat. Oscar Wilde's *The Picture of Dorian Gray* took me into a world that reminded me a bit of the Hillside's mansions, or at least of the way I imagined them to be. In Dorian's world, the rich moved through "nacre-colored" air wearing velvet dressing gowns, and their rooms were hung with oil paintings of themselves like the one of Silas Bronson that I passed on my way into the library.

The story fascinated me. Over and over I read about how Dorian's portrait grew horrible while he himself remained beautiful.

I imagined that if I could get a portrait done of me, I might avoid the liver spots and varicose veins my grandmothers had acquired. I wondered if my First Holy Communion portrait would do. It hung in our living room, a ten-by-fourteen-inch hand-colored photograph from Merideth studios in a gilt frame.

Still, a rotting portrait hidden in the attic of your house underneath a tarp was a scary proposition. It was the dark side, I'd noticed, to some things that appeared wonderful at first glance but made you think twice later. And in the quiet annex of the Waterbury library on a sunny summer day, I felt the fear that comes from knowing you'd probably do something wrong yourself if you knew you had the chance to get away with it.

How much I owed to the library and its books. We'd first met in the Brooklyn annex on our way down from Washington Avenue to Grandma's on Riverside Street. Back then, my mother had used her card to select books she thought I'd like to hear read to me.

As soon as I was old enough, Mom walked me up Church Street one day after school to the main library for my own card, number J-4912. We were expected to learn our own number by heart and to write it in pencil on a tiny line of the orange card in the book's front pocket, using a yellow pencil stub from a wooden box of them set on each of the low oak tables ringed with child-sized chairs.

Borrowing books was serious business. The librarian expected us to remove the cards from the books we'd selected and to stack them separately. Her job was to put a white card stamped with the date the book was due back into the little paper card pocket. The cards we'd removed went into the librarian's file.

Once in a while I found a book that I wanted to keep forever. *A Little Princess* by Frances Hodgson Burnett was one; *Adventures of Perrine* by Malot was another. Both books were about plucky orphans making their way against all odds. The illustrations were beautifully detailed and printed on satiny paper that I loved to run my fingers across. Befriended by both animals and adults, the heroines of these stories triumphed with happy endings.

But the library's business was lending, and there was a fine of two cents a day for late returns. And so I reluctantly brought my favorites back to Silas Bronson, allowed a decent length of time to elapse, then brought them home again, frequently rereading under the blankets by flashlight after my bedtime.

When it was my sister's turn to get her library card, I did the honors. She was as thrilled with the place as I'd been. The fact that you could take a stack of books home for two weeks at a time seemed too good to be true. We didn't merely read books; we consumed them. The first trip through the pages was a quick one to find out what happened. The second time around was for savoring the story, lingering over the details we liked best. Heroines' clothing was a favorite, as were descriptions of moral dilemmas.

If there were illustrations, the book got a third pass. Fairy tales had the most mesmerizing ones: Beauty in the rose garden with a ferocious-looking Beast in a frock coat, clearly on his best behavior was a good one, as was the stuff that flew out of the infamous box after Pandora opened it. The princess who had to kiss a frog troubled us. In the picture, she leaned against a deep dark well, her blonde hair down to the tips of her tiny shoes. Dripping at her feet was the infamous spotty frog, her golden ball in his mouth. The frog looked both smug and expectant. A prince in disguise? The author had to be kidding.

All those stories hung on a slender thread of choice. Would the heroine take a chance? How could she have enough moxie? we wondered. But then, from the perspective of the plot, how could she not? Equally puzzling as the books we read was the question of how we'd come by our love of reading.

Downstairs in our part of the house, there was only a dog-eared copy of Dr. Spock and a Bible that was mainly for display although we occasionally opened it to look at the colored pictures, termed "plates," that separated the Old Testament from the New. We'd gotten the maroon-covered book a section at a time at the A & P Market.

"Assemble Your Own Family Heirloom," the display sign had urged. And so we did, week after week, with our purchase of groceries. When your Bible was complete, the embossed end covers and colored ribbon markers attached were thrown in free of charge.

Upstairs, Grandma's house yielded a coverless copy of the *Zolar Book of Dreams*. We were particularly interested in Zolar's advice that to dream of cats meant treachery from someone whom you'd least suspect. In the bathroom closet was a heavy hard-covered green tome labeled *Medical Reference Book*. It was chock full of drawings of veins and arteries and organs in full color, not to mention the brain and also the black-and-white photos of horrible afflictions that humans might possibly get. My grandmother prized the anthology of woe as her "Dr. Book." Whenever anyone we knew was sick, we'd look up their ailment in the reference section, made grateful by the information that it wasn't us.

Our family subscribed to the morning and evening editions of the Waterbury newspaper and the *Catholic Transcript*, and my Grandmother received a periodical called the *Annals of St. Anne*. With that, they called it a day for reading. But my sister and I were always on the lookout for something to read. *Little Golden Books* from Keefe's Drugstore, Classic Comics, or any comics, from Dave's Superette, anything at our relatives' houses, we read. And when we visited our friends' houses, we read their books too while our little hostesses stood by waiting for us to finish up and play or stomped away to complain to their mothers about us.

From the first day I set foot in the Silas Bronson Library, I never ceased to be grateful to him for his bequest. Books meant I could travel in my mind to other places and times. I might look like I was sitting on the front porch of my house on Willow Street on a hot summer afternoon, my sneakered feet propped on the porch railing as I balanced the striped canvas deck chair on its back two legs. But with that stack of books beside me, I could escape heat, boredom, and the bathroom mirror's confirmation that I was chubby and had too many freckles.

"There is no frigate like a book," I read and sailed far away.

My parents, Robert Synott and Elizabeth Cremins Synott, summer 1945.

Our kitchen on Willow Street around 1952.

*Dad's workbench in the cellar on Willow Street
with the Snow White and seven Dwarfs mural above it.*

Christmas on Willow Street, 1952.

Dad's parents' bedroom and the crucifix that glowed in the dark.

My sister with our Fifties furniture and Alvin the singing chipmunk.

My cell with vanity and Hollywood bed.

*The front door at Notre Dame, nice for posing,
but all pupils came and went through the back.*

My sister Marianne, age three, on our front sidewalk.

Grandma and I on our way to St. Margaret's for Easter Mass.

Me, side yard of Willow Street. For some reason, we never took a photograph of the front of the house.

Backyard Willow Street with Grandpa raking.

Notre Dame's annual May procession. My cape was made on Grandma's Singer sewing machine.

*Kindergarten graduation. We posed with our teacher.
Of course, Grandma made my gown.*

In its heyday Notre Dame had its own notecards.

*Uniform beanie and blazer and a glimpse of the front door.
Priscilla the cat is freshly baptized.*

November, 1952. My sister's christening was an occasion worthy of the infamous horse tie. Even from this distance you can see its unique details on Dad.

Grandpa Cremins at work in Hamilton Park's fabulous rose garden.

Mom's parents, Maurice Cremins and Mary Jane O'Dwyer Cremins, in our front yard on Willow Street.

Dad's parents, Francis Synott and Dora Saunders Synott, in their backyard on Riverside Street in Brooklyn.

School

I may not have always liked the circumstance of Catholic school, the endless mountains of homework and those blue serge uniforms, but the pomp of it pleased my taste for extravaganzas. Notre Dame Academy was French for Our Lady's Academy, and so each classroom had its own statue of Mary on a pedestal at the front, to the left of the blackboard. May was Mary's month, all thirty-one days of it, and we celebrated by surrounding our statues with all the fresh flowers we could find.

"Bring them from your gardens, girls," the nuns would say. And anyone with a patch of tulips or any early-blooming flower stripped her garden bare. Our house had no garden, but we did have a lilac tree, gnarled with age, in the back by the kitchen door. On a sunny morning in May when the dew was still heavily beaded on them, I'd ask Dad to cut a bunch for me using his pocketknife on their woody stems.

He'd lay them in wet paper wrapped in a sheet of tin foil, and I'd carry them with me on the downtown bus.

"Ah, lilacs," people would remark when I boarded, juggling bookbag and bouquet as I handed the CR&L bus driver my red ticket, fished out in advance from my red leather wrist change purse. It was heart shaped with a zippered back and my name stamped on it in gold.

"They're for Our Lady," I remember telling an old woman with heavy pancake makeup. Her bright red lipstick was drawn on beyond her lips to produce a bigger mouth.

"Of course," she replied with a complicit smile and made a place for me to sit beside her on the long bench that ran down the front of the bus on either side.

One block before my stop at State Street, I'd reach up to pull the buzz cord that signaled the driver to stop. Once inside my classroom, I'd look to see who else had brought flowers. After you'd presented them to your nun for approval, you were given permission to go down the hall to the janitor's mop closet. That was where the vases were kept on shelves above the buckets and mops. My favorite one was a Roseville vase in cream and green with handles that curved back on themselves like furled leaves. It was first come first served at the mop closet, and we all were anxious to see our offerings from home displayed to their best advantage.

It was wonderful to smell the lilacs and the other flowers releasing their scents into the classroom air as the sun rose higher in the morning sky. The chalk-dust motes from the erased blackboards shimmered in the light from the windows, open since there was no air-conditioning in our school. Occasionally a bee buzzed in, perhaps as attracted as we were to Mary's bouquets, and caused the more easily alarmed among us to scream.

Screams brought a speedy lecture from our nun about God's perfect creatures and their place in our natural universe, small comfort to the girl who had one crawling across her desk or lap. "Mother" was what we called our nuns, not the more common "Sister." They came to us via the Congregation de Notre Dame's headquarters in Montreal, a place they called the Mother House.

Blessed Marguerite Bourgeois was the order's founder, and we had a special day each year when we honored her. We began by making hundreds of white construction paper daisies with yellow paper centers and pinning them to all the bulletin boards in the school. The next step was the annual reading of her life story to the whole school, assembled in the newly built auditorium. Even if you'd heard it enough to know it by heart, the highlights were still absorbing. You could almost forget the discomfort of perfect posture—which meant feet firmly planted on the floor, back straight, hands folded in your lap.

Blessed Marguerite, whose name in French meant "daisy," had been a young woman when a statue of the Blessed Mother had spoken to her.

"Go to the New World and start a school," the statue said. And so she left Troyes, France in 1653 and crossed the ocean to Canada. It was a story of Indians and pioneers packed with adventure. And although we did not know it at the time, we were connected to it by more than our school. One of our own relatives had been the first white child baptized in the New World and had been taught by Blessed Marguerite herself. If the nuns had only known of our proximity to saintliness, my sister and I would surely have gotten to kiss the relic first on her feast day.

Kissing the relic was the climax of the ceremonies honoring our founder, and it occurred after the annual procession through the school. We began in the basement's all-purpose room, grouped by grade, and worked our way to the upstairs hall where a life-sized statue of Marguerite Bourgeois looked skyward in her black gown and kerchief.

At her feet were a French settler's child and an Indian child. Mother Marguerite had a hand on each one's head. Directly in front of her stood our principal. It was her job to hold the tiny gold case that contained a relic of our founder. We'd been told that the relic held blessed bones. No one knew for sure which bones, and clearly, they were just a sample. But bones seemed awful, somehow, even if they were blessed. We approached in single file, each of us kissing the little case, and after each of us had done so, our principal dabbed at the glass with a white handkerchief to sanitize it for the next in line.

As we marched through Notre Dame in double rows heading for the relic, we sang our founder's song. It had been composed by one of our nuns and set to music, and it had dozens of verses. There were so many, in fact, that they'd been printed out for us on ditto sheets in smudgy purple ink. The chorus ran this way:

> Hail O Mother Marguerite! Bright Flame of living Charity!
> Blessed Friend of all children! Virgin Light! Vesseled in humility!

The exclamation points were to encourage us to sing with feeling. And when we were done with our ceremony, our principal dismissed us for the day with nearly the whole day free and no homework, compliments of Mother Marguerite.

Processions were a common way to honor occasions at school, and one of the prettiest came in the month of May. On a day chosen with one eye on the weather reports, we honored Mary. In our best springtime party dresses, we formed a queue and proceeded in pairs, praying the rosary on our own best rosaries, out to the courtyard behind the school. At its center on the grassy median, a life-sized statue of Mary stood with outstretched arms. There was a circular walk around the perimeter, and there we stood while an eighth-grade girl in a wedding dress and veil climbed a short ladder to crown the statue with a wreath of fresh flowers.

"Bring flowers of the fairest, bring flowers of the rarest, from garden and woodland and hillside and vale," was how the crowning ceremony song began. It seemed on target to me because it sounded like what we went through to get those bouquets for our classroom May altars.

Our families were invited to the crowning, and some mothers always cried when the bride student appeared. My own mother and both grandmothers came decked out in hats and gloves to wave discreetly to me as I passed them with folded hands and piously downcast eyes.

The red brick house at 30 Church Street where our school had begun was once a private home and a very grand one. Nearly every room had a fireplace and creamy white-paneled walls with curlicue moldings and cornices. The front hall stairs rose in a semicircular curve past a niche where the nuns had placed a statue of the Infant of Prague. On the wide landing halfway up, french doors led to a balcony with a view of the flagstone courtyard and the back door where we entered the school each morning.

Some of the downstairs rooms had cupboards secreted in the paneling that opened at a light touch in the right place. The house had twin sunporches and a butler's pantry, its multipaned windows glazed with wavy glass. The year we learned what to do if the bomb fell, my classroom was on the mansion's second floor, a room whose windows looked out onto the shady street. Our nun showed us how to get down underneath our little wooden desks and crouch there, our arms crossed over our heads as a shield. It seemed like a woefully inadequate response to the mushroom cloud I'd seen photos of in *Life* magazine, but none of us put our thoughts into words. Our uniforms were covered with chalk dust on drill days, and my mother knew without asking that we'd had a practice.

Down in the vast shadowy basement of the house was a warren of little rooms, whose past use we could only imagine. Some of them had been fitted out with pegs for our coats. The nuns called these cloakrooms. Also in the basement were our toilets, which we were told to call lavatories. And as we washed our hands at the row of little sinks with the Nile green liquid soap from the wall-mounted glass dispensers, we could look up and out through the small, high windows to see jack-in-the-pulpit unfurling along with tulips and the occasional ankle and foot of someone heading down the path to the kitchen door in back.

On sunny days, we had our recess outside in the courtyard, where the favored sport was jumping rope. But when it rained, we retreated to the basement for games such as "Farmer in the Dell," or "Wonder Ball." "Wonder Ball" made me anxious. I was wary of being "the one to hold it last," as the song went. If you were left holding the ball at the end of the song, you were out of the game and had to sit it out in the spooky basement on a bench beneath a row of coats. The bench was by the dark opening to one of the cubbies, and as I watched my classmates continue to pass the wonder ball, I tried to imagine what anyone saw in games.

In addition to our sports at NDA, the nuns ensured that we were enriched on a weekly basis by lessons in elocution, music, and art. Art was taught each week by a diminutive nun with a black moustache. Mother was a good sport and nothing fazed her.

"Well, now," was all she'd say when confronted by a drawing of a crooked tree or a bird with its crayoned beak out of whack.

"Well, now. Look at this." Mother gave an annual prize at the year's end to the girl with the cleanest crayon box. The boxes were flat metal cigar boxes from who knows where. They each held eight fat, stubby crayons lacking their paper wraps. One year I won at last by sacrificing my flowered handkerchief to scrub my tin's lining to a brilliant shine.

Music day meant that the music teacher was traveling across town on foot from Catholic High. A small brown wooden organ on wheels was pushed into our classroom by two girls who vied for the weekly honor, and the blackboard, in short order, was covered with drawings of notes and staffs and G clefs.

"La-la-la-LA-la-la-la," we sang on an ascending scale. Our music nun had once taught young Rosalind Russell, and it was said that she'd known from the start that the girl from Cracker Hill had what it takes for stardom.

Elocution was the most unusual of our weekly enrichments. It was provided by a lay teacher, a genteel Southern lady of middle age with hennaed hair and a green celluloid eyeshade like one I'd seen in a picture at a great-uncle's house of dogs playing poker. Our teacher wore tailored suits in gray or black and sensible oxford shoes, and her voice was always gentle and well modulated. "Well modulated" meant that although her voice was low, you could still hear her clearly across a crowded auditorium if she told you to mind your manners.

Our teacher taught us to curtsey, drawing our skirts wide in our two hands, the toe of one shoe slightly behind the heel of the other as we sank gracefully, heads inclined toward our audience, a pleasant smile on our faces, but never a grin.

"I shall read for you a poem entitled . . . ," we intoned as a preface to our solo recitals.

"Poy-em, girls. Not poe-em," our teacher coached softly. Practice made us perfect at Joyce Kilmer's "Trees" and "Paul Revere's Ride" by Henry Wadsworth Longfellow, and our recitals were given drama by the broad gestures she deemed suited to our material.

When the entire class performed Whittier's "Barbara Frietchie," our program was considered to be thrilling. Half of us took the part of Barbara herself. The other half was General Stonewall Jackson. The narrative of the story line we said in unison:

> "Shoot if you must, this old gray head,
> But spare your country's flag," she said.

That was my group's part. We said it in squeaky, high voices as the soprano part because we were using what our teacher called choral speech. We spoke the lines holding our right hands over our hearts.

"Who touches a hair of yon gray head
Dies like a dog! March on!" he said.

That was the other group's reply, given in a growly alto voice, pantomiming upraised swords. A Southern belle herself, displaced by widowhood and circumstance to our Northern mill town, our teacher clearly had favored the Grey in the War Between the States although she explained to us that she could see both sides of the story.

My class grew fond of curtseying. We used it even on the milkman when he made his daily delivery of thirty-two waxed cardboard pint-sized cartons of white milk to our classroom to wash down the sandwiches we brought from home to eat at our desks.

"Good morning, Mr. Mooney," we chorused to the man from Knudsen's Dairy.

It was an elegant education for a girl from a blue-collar Waterbury family. My own parents were the only ones from their respective families who had graduated from high school, and my sister's and my presence at Notre Dame Academy was a privilege that sprang from my parents' hopes for us as well as their hard work. Looking back, I see it was an education tailored to what we might become in the American Dream rather than who we were in the 1950s on Cracker Hill.

And as I practiced my penmanship in the Palmer Method workbook, carefully copying in cursive script the poem by Wordsworth that began with the following lines:

> Under a spreading chestnut tree
> The village smithy stands;

I daydreamed about how I might one day sign my name with a flourish in a book I had written that might achieve greatness, which in my eyes was a place on the annex shelves of the Silas Bronson Library.

Horses

"What do you want to be when you grow up?" was a question grown-ups liked to ask. Perhaps it was a game to them, but to me it felt like a pop quiz where I needed to come up with the right answer, fast. The people who asked me usually worked in factories or in downtown stores, jobs they'd probably never dreamed of themselves as children. Their question seemed to imply that for my generation the sky was the limit.

A career looked far away to me, a speck on the horizon. In my family, the career women were nurses with starched white uniforms and jaunty caps that indicated from which hospital school they'd graduated. On television, I saw situation comedy secretaries, whom I admired for their typing tours de force and for the way they could handle their cranky bosses and manipulate them into doing things that came out right in the end. The laughs came because the secretary's way was inevitably the right way all along, the boss being the bumbler. It made me wonder why those clever women weren't bosses themselves.

Occasionally one of our nuns would suggest that I might have a vocation. That was a scary thought, that the calling to be a nun might creep up behind me and seize control like a deus ex machina grabbing the wheel of an airplane and flying me to the Mother House in Montreal, Canada, before I knew what had hit me.

"You read a lot. Maybe you can be a teacher," was a suggestion I often heard. It was true that I sometimes played school, handing out piles of homework to my imaginary students. But that was more a desire to see what it felt like to be on the other end of the stick than an indication of a true calling to the field of education.

What I really wanted to be when I grew up was a cowgirl. I saw myself so clearly out West among the purple sage, riding a pinto pony in my fringed buckskin vest and chaps. Each Saturday morning for a number of years, I rehearsed my part in front of Grandma's small screen black-and-white TV. Outside the windows, neighbors on Willow Street went their merry way doing chores like washing cars and mowing lawns. But inside, I strapped on my holster belt with matching cap pistols, tightened the cord on my cowboy hat, and joined my pals.

Hopalong Cassidy was my hands down favorite, a good guy who wore black. It made a nice contrast with his white hair and with Topper, his magical white horse. Topper had saved Hoppy's life, rescuing him from a fire, and he also knew a lot of tricks. I knew this because I had Hoppy and all the other TV cowboys on my Viewmaster reels, fourteen views per little round card. That was how I also knew that Gene Autry's shirt was red and his horse, Champion, a honey brown.

Gene was one of the singing cowboys, and I knew something important about him that no one else had seemed to figure out. Every single Saturday, Gene, moseying along on Champion, would burst into song. And every single week, just as the last note of his song had died away, someone would shoot at him and knock his white hat off. Why he couldn't make the connection, I didn't understand. I wished I could send him a telegram: either don't sing this week or duck when you are through.

I swallowed my Westerns whole, not troubling to question the difference in time periods. The Lone Ranger existed in the West of stagecoaches and Indian attacks while Sky King and his niece Penny flew above it in an airplane called the *Songbird*. Perhaps the reason they seemed to coexist so easily in my mind was because my own world was a combination of the old and the new, the difference between the end of the forties and the new decade of the fifties.

In my neighborhood, prewar cars in basic black with running boards hugged the streets alongside postwar models with tail fins in pastel colors like pink and blue or even racy red. A few aunts still had Andrews Sisters' hairdos and dresses with shoulder pads, quite a contrast to the ones with the Dior New Look of wasp waists and long, full skirts.

Living rooms filled with doily-laden suites of furniture were invaded by modern blonde wood tables and draperies in atomic prints. And the plastic that so delighted me in my Woolworth's toys was everywhere, from ashtrays to pocketbooks, all marked Made in Japan.

In 1949 when we'd moved to Willow Street, I'd been treated to the sight of an iceman delivering a huge dripping block held with tongs to a Victorian house across the street. And occasionally early on a spring morning before traffic got going, I'd seen a man drive up the hill in an open cart pulled by one brown horse.

"Rags, rags," he'd cried, looking for neighborhood women to sell him their old clothes. Most magical of all, in the early fifties, a man from somewhere in Overlook who kept a horse and sleigh would ride down Willow Street late at night as the snow fell, the jingle from his horse's harness bells the only sound.

The bulk of my horseback riding had taken place at Lake Quassapaug Amusement Park's carousel, where I favored the wild maned jumpers with glass eyes in the outside row. For the real thing, I relied on the Pine Drive-In movie theater in the twilight hour that preceded the show. Dad's parents were open-air aficionados. We'd arrive early to grab our favorite spot near the concession stand and ladies room. Grandma then rolled down her car window, hooked the speaker box on to it, and pushed the button to be sure it worked. Once that was over, we'd head down to the area beneath the big white screen. That was where the horses waited to give rides.

The drive-in horses had backs as wide as my Hollywood bed, or so it seemed. The handler obliged with a leg up into the creaking leather saddle that was never cinched quite tight enough to stay level. Clinging to its pommel, I'd roll like a ship in heavy seas as we made two slow circles around the makeshift ring. It would have been nice to have had a mount with some pep, but even though I clicked my tongue encouragingly and dug my heels surreptitiously into the horse's sides, rattling the tooled Western-style stirrups that looked like giant fortune cookies, not one horse ever so much as raised its head, let alone broke into a gallop for the hills of Wolcott, one town over.

Given my interest in horses, the gift I found for Father's Day one year was perfect. Up the street from us on Willow was a tiny sliver of a shop in the building that housed Dave's Superette. It had a stamp-sized vestibule, a brown linoleum counter, and on the other side of the counter, a man who repaired shoes. I don't recall that we ever took our shoes to him. My family preferred the Olympia Shoe Repair downtown on East Main Street, where you could sit in disposable brown paper slippers in a little booth with a wooden half door while your shoes were heeled and buffed. But this neighborhood shop had something special, a window display of a rack of ties.

The hand-lettered sign read the following:

Previously Owned Ties
$1.00 Each, Guaranteed

And mixed in with the predictable striped and patterned ones was a tie no one could miss. It was satin and wide. Gleaming on it was a hunting scene. Men on horseback in red coats were pictured chasing a bushy-tailed orange fox across a lime green field. Black-and-white spotted dogs ran behind the fox, their open mouths showing their lolling tongues. Up close, the detail was amazing. I could even see the whites of the horses' eyes.

"I'll be right back," I called to the shoemaker. "Don't sell this tie while I'm gone."

On the shelf above our kitchen sink stood my blue plastic piggy bank with eyes that wiggled when you shook it. If you flipped Mr. Pig upside down and stuck a table knife into the slit on his back, it was possible to extract any amount of coins stashed inside for safekeeping. Retrieving a dollar was the work of a moment.

The shoemaker put my purchase in a creased brown grocery bag for me to carry it home. I tucked it into my bottom bureau drawer next to my patent leather purse and white cardigan with the little satin roses down the front.

That year, I had the perfect Father's Day gift. I could hardly wait for Dad to open my present. How surprised my mother and grandparents looked when he held the tie up. In the sunlight, its colors were even more vivid. Dad laughed as he tried it on and thanked me. Since he climbed telephone poles for a living, I knew the tie would have to wait for a special occasion. And when it did come out of the closet, for a christening or to a play at school, it was clear it was one of a kind from the comments it drew. Dad always explained that I'd chosen it. But even if its admirers had gone to the same store as I had, they'd have been out of luck because there never was another tie like that in its window, though I looked in every time I passed by.

Around Town

Sometimes after supper in the time before I could read to myself, I rendezvoused with Grandpa on his kitchen platform rocker. *Uncle Arthur's Bedtime Stories* were what we read, working our way through all five volumes. It seems the books were unique to our house. None of my classmates had ever heard of them, and once they'd been briefed on their contents, none of them cared to hear more.

But to me, the stories were fascinating. The covers of the books were embossed in gold with a drawing of a seated boy and girl held spellbound by an open book, presumably the *Stories*. The design was completed by a lighted candle at each end of the title. Uncle Arthur's tales covered decades. The earliest were set in the twenties, others during the Depression, the most recent in the forties, some during World War II.

Most took place in England. Later on, Uncle Arthur seemed to have visited California. But no matter where the author hung his hat, the stories kept to their point: be good. From Bible stories to domestic incidents, good children were rewarded, and bad ones got their comeuppance. I'd already discovered that the real world was not fair, and so I found the world of Uncle Arthur particularly satisfying. As to the occasional situation where I disagreed with the black or white morality presented without a shade of gray, I learned to hold the mental reservation that in my case things would be different, early practice for grown-up rationalization.

Before diving into our volume of choice, Grandpa and I fortified ourselves with peanut-cluster candies, odd-shaped lumps of peanuts bound together with milk chocolate. Instructive tales always seemed more palatable on a full stomach. The books had become mine courtesy of Dad's mother via a door-to-door salesman. I doubt Grandma knew she was buying thinly disguised morality stories and Protestant ones to boot. I imagine she was impressed by the elegance of the five hardbound volumes in red, green, orange, blue, and brown; and dazzled afterward by the classy way they looked lined up on her mahogany cedar chest in the front hall. But I know that it was having those peculiar books on hand upstairs in our house that made me eager to decipher for myself the stories that accompanied the intriguing black-and-white photos of temptations, tornados, and other of life's challenges.

In the green volume, I was drawn to a picture of sweet-faced Jesus with hair longer than my mother would ever have allowed me to wear mine. He was surrounded by children in modern-day garb vying for a seat on his lap.

"Suffer the little children to come unto me," Mark 10:14 read the caption. "Suffering" was what Dad called it when he sat up all night in the kitchen rocker nursing a migraine headache. It was a word I associated with hot-water bottles and the smell of Musterole Rub, and I couldn't see how it applied to children.

"Behold I stand at the door and knock," Revelation 3:20 read another caption, this one beneath a picture of Jesus in a billowing cape. He was tapping at the door of a vine-covered cottage on a dark night. You could see that the wind was blowing the ivy backward, and that it was pretty cold outside.

"Why don't they open the door?" I always asked. "If they looked out and saw the halo, I bet they'd open it right away."

"Do you want me to read this or not?" was the way Grandpa usually persuaded me to be quiet.

Inside the covers of Uncle Arthur's books faith worked for believers in the same way that magic wands worked in fairy tales for wizards: a starving family knelt to pray for food. Suddenly the mother felt something underneath her knee. It proved to be a twenty-dollar bill. Another family was on the way to Bible camp when the old jalopy blew a tire. In the desert they, too, knelt to pray. And when they opened their eyes, in the ditch beside them was a brand-new tire, just the right size for their car.

No matter how much time I spent on my knees, a pony never materialized. But mine was a small disappointment compared to the case of *Doreen's Jewel Box*. Doreen had asked for one for her birthday, but received a Bible instead. It had a pretty white cover, but disappointed Doreen threw it across the room in a fit of pique. That led to a lecture on vanity, and a quote from Proverbs 31:10 about a virtuous woman being hard to find but worth more than rubies. The story continued in that vein, jewel analogies in the Bible being offered in lieu of dime store baubles, Doreen's dream of pearls countered with the quote of heaven as the one pearl of great price.

The story concluded with a chastened Doreen hugging her book as she saw the light. How grateful I was that the women in my family liked costume jewelry, because I liked the sparkling bangles and brooches myself and would have been equally crushed to have woken up to the same situation on my own birthday.

Grandpa's favorite story was called "Knocking the *T* out of 'Can't,'" a "pull yourself up by your own bootstraps" tale of hard work. Grandma, who'd once lived on a farm, favored the tale of a farm boy who was asked by the farmer to tell what kind of worker he was. The lad enigmatically—and annoyingly, as far as I was concerned—would only repeat that he could sleep on windy nights. When the inevitable big storm came, it was discovered that the boy could sleep because he'd done his work so well that nothing at all was blown away.

The worst possible of storms, a tornado, was illustrated in the brown book by a malevolent black funnel cloud twirling toward a cluster of tiny houses. Inside one of them, the family knelt to pray. And, concluded the story, theirs was the only house left standing when the storm had passed.

Around the same time as I was reading these stories, a billboard appeared on the banks of the Naugatuck River across from the Tranquility Farm Dairy Bar on South Main Street, where my grandparents liked to go for ice cream. They preferred to get the sundaes to go and eat them in the car. Sitting in the backseat of Grandpa's green Chevy spooning hot fudge, I had ample time to study the billboard closely.

In its center, a white-robed Mary appeared on a cloud to three kneeling children clutching rosaries. My grandmother explained that Mary was the Lady of Fatima and that her message to the world was the following: "The family that prays together stays together."

In school, the nuns, too, had explained that praying the rosary might be the only way to spare our country from Communism, the same threat that kept us scrambling beneath our desks at a moment's notice for air raid drills. I could see more and more that the world was a risky place.

Also on the far bank of the Naugatuck River were huge twin silver spheres like giant's toys. They had ladders that went all the way up their sides to the catwalks on top. The balls were filled with natural gas, the same stuff that popped into a blue flame when we turned on our stoves and that could and did frequently burn the hair off the arm of whoever had to light the oven's broiler.

South of the balls was a brick building with a tiny light burning at the top of it that, according to local lore, functioned as a pilot light. People said that if the little light ever went out, it would mean that the entire Naugatuck Valley was about to explode.

"Don't get nervous," Grandpa assured me. "We'd head for the hills." But I didn't think his car could go fast enough. As I saw it, tornadoes, gas explosions, air raid drills, and Communism were all tied in together. And clearly, the only way out was for me to get my mother and father to join me in the living room for a nightly rosary.

My parents surprised me by failing to draw the same conclusion. They decided to humor me for one night, shifting their knees on the scratchy rose-patterned wool rug as we gathered around the hassock in a little circle. I'd expected to feel holy, but I felt self-conscious, and after kneeling upright through five decades of Hail Marys, I was more than a bit uncomfortable. The decision to end our sessions was mutual.

"We'll light some candles on Sunday in church," my mother offered as an alternative.

Another reminder of life's dangers came when Grandpa read to me, following the words with the index finger of his right hand. The middle finger next to it was missing its tip right down to the first joint. Grandpa had caught it under a barrel at work when he was a boy. The oldest of five children, he'd been made to quit school to help support the family, staying only long enough to learn to read and write.

"Did you mind?" I asked. But he never answered.

Having Dad's parents upstairs was like having access to a second set of parents, unusually indulgent ones. Grandma was a particularly good companion, which was lucky for me because of the edict that most neighborhood children were off-limits. My school let out before theirs, so I was back home in time to watch them struggle down Willow Street in groups of two and three, the boys roughhousing or calling to each other in a way my mother called "common."

I'd never been inside the Driggs public school, but I had visited St. Margaret's to prepare for my First Holy Communion. I'd found it overwhelming, simply because it was busier and bigger than I was used to. The nun in charge, whom the pupils called "Sister," ordered me to the front of the room and told me to curtsey so the others could see how we did things at Notre Dame. Afterward, I'd been called "stuck up" by my fellow communion goers as I slunk back to my seat.

Activities with Grandma were of a practical nature. She'd listen to my recitations of the homework we were required to memorize, and work out the long division and multiplication problems that I found vexing. When I'd done with mine, I'd go into her bedroom where she'd placed the correct answers underneath the bedroom phone and see how far off the mark I'd gone

When Grandma cooked, I watched, admiring her firm hand blending the meatloaf ingredients and the way she could separate an apple from its peel in one long unbroken spiral. Watching her sew was another spectator sport. First, the walnut cabinet with the diamond-shaped inlay of lighter wood in its door was opened, and the black Singer machine popped up from its hiding place where it hung upside down like a bat. The machine had gold squiggles decorating every available surface.

This machine had produced my christening gown with matching coat and hat that now lived in tissue paper in the cedar chest, along with my white organdy kindergarten graduation gown and matching drawstring bag. Party dresses and sundresses embellished with the buttonhole and the ruffle attachments as well as my annual Halloween costume came courtesy of Mr. Singer and Grandma. One favorite costume was a reproduction of Snow White's costume, complete with cape. All I'd lacked that year had been the seven dwarfs. Another had been a princess costume that entailed Dad's effort for the megaphone-shaped gold hat with trailing scarf. After that one, I was strongly encouraged to lay off the fairy tales for inspiration.

Grandma's sewing included the dolls' clothes, Ginny's in particular. Coats and a peignoir set for eight-inch Ginny were surpassed only by two knitted dresses, one with a matching muff no bigger that half of my little fingernail yet somehow fully lined in satin. Perhaps it was watching my grandmother churn these things out so effortlessly that gave me the idea that I, too, might have a talent for sewing.

Across the Waterbury Green on the opposite side from Notre Dame lay the Waterbury Girls' Club. 35 Park Place was its address, and Waterburians were proud to say that ours was the first club in the nation, our town its Connecticut birthplace. Tucked away behind the Masonic Temple and the Standard Taxi building, the club's small white house was set like a lady's lacy handkerchief in the pocket of a man's business suit. Its white-pillared Greek revival porch gave me the illusion of being Scarlett O'Hara at a downsized Tara.

Some of my classmates went there after school, and when I heard about the sewing lessons, I went too. Inside the Girls' Club, every inch of space was put to use. The basement housed ceramics, the second floor, art. The main floor had the kitchen, where girls in aprons cut out endless sugar cookies with a glass turned upside down. The middle room there, the former parlor, was my room, the room where the sewing machines held sway.

The neatly spaced rows of varnished oak machines all had treadles that required foot pumping. The girls behind them worked intently, heads down, their back and forth treadling as fervent as novena prayers. The only sound in the room was the whir of the machines. This room was presided over by an instructor who was a legend, spoken of in low tones of respect.

I'd had a few lessons from Grandma, but her machine and I hadn't hit it off. I'd kept getting the tension tight and ending up with a ball of thread on the back side of the cloth. I'd imagined the Girls' Club machines would be easier on me, but I'd imagined wrong. Beginners traditionally started off with an apron. The fabric I'd chosen was a busy little sprigged cotton print of red flowers on a yellow background.

Working the treadle in an even rhythm while guiding the fabric in a straight line at the same time was as beyond me as the task of the princess in *Rumplestilskin*, who'd been asked to spin flax into gold. Each week our instructor inspected my work and then said, "Rip it out and start again."

The girls I'd come with moved on to other projects that winter: skirts, and as it grew warmer, shorts. My apron, a full one with a neck hole, had lost its clean, crisp finish by the time it met my teacher's standards at long last. But when I tried it on for the first time, I found I'd grown too tall for my head to fit through the apron's neckpiece. There really was only one reply possible from the instructor when she saw the situation. Of course her solution was, "Rip it out and start again."

I traveled home on the Overlook bus from Girls' Club with a quieter crowd than the usual one directly after the city schools let out. Those earlier busses were always filled with high school students. They took over the entire back section as if they owned it, lolling comfortably on the wide seat that went across the back. On report card day, they worked intently back there, signing each other's report cards if needed or sometimes even changing grades so their parents wouldn't have fits. I wondered how they could do it well enough to avoid detection, but their confidence led me to conclude that they were as skilled at their forgeries as the men Jack Webb hunted each week on *Dragnet*.

As my bus approached the corner of Willow and Ridgewood, I'd stand and pull the cord to signal my stop. Dragging my bookbag, I'd head up the walk to our front door. Inside, I'd shuck my uniform jumper and white blouse, the hated brown oxfords and blue clip on tie. When I heard Jack Bailey bellow his standard TV game show question: "Would YOU like to be queen for a day?" I'd run upstairs to Grandma's parlor for a show that never failed to amaze me.

The winner each day was the woman with the worst hard-luck story. Lumpy, careworn housewives in tatty cotton housedresses told Jack Bailey about fires and floods, deserting husbands, and desperately needed operations. When all of them were through, the audience voted as Jack stood behind each contestant in turn and held his hand above her head. The camera would then pan to the applause meter to show its wildly jumping needle on the gauge. The meter had the last word that made the winner official. The queen got a golden crown, an ermine-trimmed cape, and a lot of new appliances.

After "*Queen for a Day*" came "*The Big Payoff*," hosted by former Miss America Bess Meyerson. On this show, the woman contestant started off on the throne. Her boyfriend stood beside her, fielding questions. If he got the questions wrong, down she got from the throne and no prizes, including the coveted mink coat. I wondered what happened when the losers got together out of camera range.

"No doubt the fur will fly," was Grandma's cryptic answer. It sounded as if it would be something worth seeing, if only we could. But other people's bids for fame and fortune were on the far side of the TV tube until the next afternoon, and the clock said it was time to think of dinner.

Dinner at our house was as predictable as time and tide. The time was five when Dad and Grandpa returned from work. As to the menu, I could tell the day of the week by what was on the table. Sunday was the roast, segueing into Monday's hash. Tuesday was liver, a dish no amount of bacon could make palatable to my sister or to me. Wednesday brought chicken, and Thursday, meatloaf. Friday was problematic because none of us liked fish, and to eat meat on Friday was the pathway to hell.

And so to save us from mortal sin, Dad brought home a cheese pizza from Domenic's on Wolcott Street each Friday, collecting it on his way back from the Southern New England Telephone Company's Lakewood Road garage. Saturday was not as firmly on the map as the other days. Perhaps my mother would decide to make spaghetti and meatballs, its sauce simmering all day with an aroma that tempted us to dart into the kitchen for a taste, a small one, but one that needed to be repeated again and again.

Grandma, in cold weather, sometimes fried dough, a cauldron of boiling oil bubbling up the lumpy treats she called "cry babies." On summer nights, we often coaxed our parents into a ride to Blackie's hot dog stand. When we reached it, way out on East Main Street, it was a sure thing that my sister would ask to have her hot dog peeled and that Dad would always oblige.

On our rides, we sometimes saw families who'd brought their real dogs along, holding on to them as they hung their heads out the window, tongues flapping in the breeze, punctuated by the occasional frenzied bark. We'd had a dog, too, for a year or so. He was a black cocker spaniel named Sooty, duly registered with the American Kennel Club as ours. I don't recall that my sister or I had ever asked for a dog. We were happy with our cats. Yet one Sunday evening when I returned from a weekend with Mom's parents, there he was on the back porch eating puppy food, his curly ears tied back by my mother with a ribbon bow.

Sooty grew quickly into a problem twice his size. He loved to run away, favoring excursions through heavy traffic to the other side of Willow Street, then heading south. When captured and tied, he'd lie next to us on the front porch, evenings, still as a lawn ornament unless someone walked past the house. A low growl for man, woman, or child was the very least he could do; and we learned to live with it. But Sooty was a dog of opinions, and his particular nemeses were two: a handicapped child and an old lady with bulging varicose veins. Snarling and lunging, he'd leap from the porch. If you were the one whose chair had his leash tethered to it, you'd be in for a ride.

Dad's fear of a lawsuit was greater than our hope that Sooty, curled by the kitchen radiator at night like a model pet, might change. And so my mother phoned in an ad to the Waterbury paper.

"One AKC pedigreed black cocker spaniel. Male. Excellent disposition. Free to a good home in the country."

Within a week, Sooty had moved to Middlebury. I'd read most of Albert Payson Terhune's series chronicling the famous Collie, *Lad of Sunnybank*, and I consoled myself by imagining our former pet frolicking in open fields that stretched for miles.

Except for the occasional wild card like our dog experiment, our days continued in a routine of school and church, meals, and family visits that made my growing up feel protected and secure. It wasn't that there was never anything to worry about, but rather that I felt sure that whatever came up, the grown-ups would be able to fix it.

It never occurred to me that as I was growing older, my parents and grandparents were too. And I never imagined that the cars we watched wending their way along Willow Street in ever-increasing numbers night and day were making it easier to get out of Waterbury to the country, or at least to the neighboring towns where shiny new ranch houses purchased with the GI Bill by Dad's contemporaries had begun to make Cracker Hill's triple-deckers a neighborhood of rapid turnover and change.

One good thing about our family was that we were seldom sick, except for commonplace complaints for my sister and me like chicken pox, measles, and mumps. At those times, my mother's nursing skills made convalescence a pleasure. Fresh nightgowns and fluffed pillows, the green wooden bed tray painted with water lilies, and pudding still warm from its pan were heaven; and we prolonged those sick days home from school as long as we could.

Dad's main complaint was migraines, but his parents' pains were more nebulous. Whatever they were, the smells of Vicks, Musterole, and Ben-Gay wafted daily on the air of the second floor. Perhaps that was what gave Grandma the idea to purchase her own diathermy to have on hand for twenty-four-hour call. What it looked like was a large black box with heavy metal clasps to hold it shut and a big black handle for easy lifting. When not in use, it lived in a front room closet beneath Grandpa's suit and topcoat. But often as not, the diathermy was set up in the living room by an armchair.

All our household, and relatives as well, were invited to use it, though there were few takers. Grandma and Daddy used it voluntarily while my sister and I were strapped in without being given a choice. Mom and Grandpa declined. Although Grandma thought highly of her device, we seemed to be the only ones who'd ever heard of it, let alone had one in their closet.

What the diathermy did was a mystery to me. Days when Grandma set it up, Grandpa would be heard to mutter

"Quack, quack," referring sotto voce to the doctor who'd convinced Grandma to buy it. He'd also said on the day it was delivered, "There's a sucker born every minute."

I knew he was quoting P. T. Barnum, the Park City circus man who'd brought the world General Tom Thumb. Why Grandma's machine should have a connection to a midget was beyond me. My grandmother was barely five feet tall, but when I asked if the diathermy would make her grow, she gave me what we called one of her "dirty looks" and sent me downstairs to my mother.

The way the machine worked was through electricity. You'd lay one of the heavily weighted rubber pads on the part that ailed you, throw switch, and let the current rip. A violet line appeared then in the diathermy's glass window gauge. It was round like a port in Captain Nemo's submarine *Nautilus* in Jules Verne's *Twenty Thousand Leagues Under the Sea*.

Strapped into Grandpa's armchair, I'd wait for something to happen: for smoke to pour from the box, for my hair to stand on end, or simply for the pads to cause some kind of sensation somewhere. But all there ever was was a businesslike hum from its motor as the inscrutable diathermy went about its work.

Grandma's black box was far from the only thing in town that smacked to me of a science fiction novel. I found it even more implausible that flowing beneath Waterbury's streets was a buried river. Up in the north end of town flanking Lakewood Road were two lakes. The one called Lakewood had a tiny island thought by some people to occasionally change position, and on the lawn beside it, a pavilion that had once housed a carousel.

The other lake, Bellview, was where Great Brook began, meandering down through the heart of town. Its burial took place in the vicinity of Vine Street. From there, it headed toward East Main Street and along Brook Street to enter the Naugatuck River at last at Bank Street.

Stories I'd been told about the construction of Great Brook's conduit included carefully laid, vaulted brick ceilings and sections with granite walls. The subterranean channel sounded like what I'd learned in geography about Egypt's pyramids: grandly constructed tombs that no one's eyes would see. Why, I wondered, had the little river been buried? The answer I was given was simply that it had been in Waterbury's way.

Equally fascinating to me because of its name was the Mad River. Coursing out of Scovill's Dam in Wolcott, it, too, ended in the Naugatuck. While not exactly angry, the Mad River was definitely frenetic. It seemed to rush everywhere. It went under Meriden Road and East Main Street, down past the Scovill Mill, then on to Mill Street and South Main. Mornings on the bus to Notre Dame, I often sat with a woman whose fiance was a member of the Mad River Grange. I'd always assumed that granges were places out west somewhere where farmers met to argue about grazing sheep versus cattle on the range, and so I was nonplussed to learn that an organization I'd associated with cowboy movies and range wars had an arm in the Brass City, in a small wooden building out on Meriden Road.

Even though the Mad River and Great Brook had served the city's manufacturing, it hadn't been all work and no play for them. Bellview Lake had once boasted a pavilion and boats to rent, and Lakewood, a small amusement park. Scovill's Dam still had a beach where off-duty employees could go to swim, and my mother had gone there summer Sundays when her father and uncles were Scovill men.

There were Scovill houses, too, although none of my family had ever lived in them. Once I'd had a teacher who'd lived in one, a regal lady with purple-rinsed hair. Sometimes we'd drive her home after a school event, waving good-bye as she stepped out in front of the white picket fence that demarcated her house from all of the others lined up in row upon row of brick buildings between Wood Street and Ives, deep in the inner city's heart north of Scovill's.

Shade trees and beds of flowers in their tidy front yards softened them, making each unit distinct from its fellows, and their varied roof lines were charming. But still, they were packed together like the picture I'd seen of the row house where my grandparents had lived in Burry Port, Wales, during Grandpa's coal-miner days en route to America. My grandparents, though, insisted that they were first-rate little places with light, heat, and running water—all the amenities of the time—and light-years away from some of the other places that workers might have had to call home without the company's help.

White City's collection of freestanding houses off East Main Street looked more inviting to me, perhaps because their street layout and front lawns gave them a more suburban, *"Father Knows Best"* ambiance. Taking their name from the fact that they were all, at one time, painted white, they'd been built for workers at American Brass.

I thought about those two sections of town, brand-new at the time the mills were churning out goods for the Great War, and wondered how the people had gotten back and forth to their jobs in a time before everyone had a car.

"Shank's mare," was what Grandpa said he and his siblings had used, an alternative to a trolley. Pushing her babies in a carriage, Dad's mother had walked from Riverside Street to a factory on South Main for buttons to hand sew onto cards back home at her kitchen table. Grandpa's sisters had walked to work at the box shop or the clock shop, and my mother's family, to Scovill's. To them, it was just the way things were. Still, when I pictured them walking back and forth in winter ice storms or in the dog days of August, I saw that there had been nothing picturesque about the good old days from that perspective.

Near the turnoff for White City out on East Main Street was the brick fortress where Waterbury's own Chief Two Moon had concocted his magical elixirs. On the shelf in her furnace room, my mother's mother had a dusty cardboard box that had once housed a bottle of his Bitter Oil. On it was a picture of the chief in full Indian regalia, buckskinned and war bonneted, standing cross-armed above twin moons. One moon was drawn frowning, the other smiling, presumably illustrating before and after the tonic's use. And even though the chief himself was long gone from Waterbury, twin bas-relief chiefs on his building's facade still observed East Main Street and its goings-on.

A few blocks beyond the chief's former store lay Calvary Cemetery, and across the street from it, the billboard of Little Miss Sunbeam, offering everyone who looked her way a slice of batter-whipped white bread. Just behind her lay the Reymond's Bakery, home of the bread that was a staple in many Waterbury homes including ours. On occasion, the company held a contest for Little Miss

Dory Fitzgerald

Carol & Jeanne,

Thought you'd enjoy this memoire of young girl growing up in Waterbury in 1950s.

Reminded me of BLTs at the Elton and many more adventures with Barry clan.

Lots of Love
Dory

Sunbeam look-alikes, and every freckle faced, curly-haired little girl in the city was urged to enter.

My mother's parents lived in the east end, heading toward the Prospect side of it, in a housing project off Hamilton Avenue. The first unit in the first building was 21 Rawley Avenue, the end one opposite an undeveloped area we thought of as woods. From the four-paned window in their white front door, I looked across into a dense copse of trees with a huge maple at its center. It was a tree that looked old enough to have been around when Waterbury was still known as Mattatuck. Though the woods also had a rusty set of metal pipes known as "monkey bars" for children to play on, I never saw a child anywhere in sight. In fact, the metal hoops and bars had the look of something left by a previous civilization, the kind of thing an archeologist might come upon while scouting in a jungle.

The contrast between the crowded housing complex where my grandparents lived and the thicket adjacent to it gave me the feeling that this part of town was poised either to expand or to revert to nature at a moment's notice.

Inside my grandparents' house, there was also a sense of things in transition, but this was due to my grandmother's style of keeping house. The order that held sway on Willow Street was upended across town by domestic arrangements more in the style of *Alice in Wonderland*. Grandma kept her earrings and brooches in the pantry's teacups and her hairnets, lipstick, and rouge on the coal bin's broad lid across from the furnace. The idea that anything could land anywhere was anarchy to my mother, but a delight to my sister and me.

New things and old ones coexisted amicably at Grandma's. In the parlor, a crank-up Victrola and its seventy-eight records stood next to the tiny black-and-white, rabbit-eared TV. Her marble-topped table cozied up to a fifties vinyl couch and chair beneath the huge hand-colored photographs of Killarney's upper and middle lakes. For a number of years before it self-destructed in a puff of smoke, the kitchen boasted the oldest living toaster, an appliance with twin chrome trap doors that pulled down to reveal slices of bread blackened by the red-hot coils.

Anything given to my grandparents deliberately or left at their house by accident remained there. Christmas cards and lists of addresses, a songbook of Irish favorites though none of us could read music, stacks of gauzy tieback curtains and their plastic pushpins shaped like little dogs or flower pots—all found homes in various cupboards or in the doorless closets behind cretonne curtains in faded floral prints. And there were books in my grandparents' house, tucked in drawers and closets in a haphazard fashion. My mother's fourth-grade *Cathedral Basic Reader* and a copy of Thornton Burgess's *Adventures of Johnny Chuck* were in the furnace room. Mom's home economics' cookbook, *All About Home Baking,* lived in the closet of the bedroom I called mine.

"The woman who is too busy to bother to sift," I read, "may easily put too much flour into her cake—and ruin it!" The house also held a copy of S. S. Van

Dine's *The Greene Murder Case*, a puzzling story both because of its five-syllable words and also because of its copious footnotes written in foreign languages. But the home run book, as far as I was concerned, was the tattered paperback copy of *Back Street* by Fannie Hurst. Its heroine was involved with a married man.

"I know I walk the backstreets of your life," she whined to him. This was a book I read at night after my grandparents had gone to sleep. I never asked how this motley collection of literature had come to Rawley Avenue. Perhaps my grandfather had collected them from the park's lost and found, or maybe someone at school had given them to my mother. Not knowing their origin made the books more interesting to me, like flotsam washed ashore from a distant wreck in time.

On the second floor of my grandparents' house opening off a long, narrow hall were three bedrooms and a bath. Grandma had the front room with a matching walnut veneer bedroom suite and two windows looking east toward Hamilton Park. Grandpa's had a view of the woods and an amazing collection of holy pictures and plaster statuary. There was a two-by-three-feet lithograph on tin of St. Therese with eyes that seemed to follow me around the room, a picture of Pope Pius XII, a dresser top shrine with dozens of little statues ranging from St. Anne to Our Lady of Fatima, a red glass votive holder, a stack of candles, and a large box of Ohio Blue Tip matches. My job, on weekends I was in residence, was to dust and rearrange the collection, and I often wondered what it was that my grandfather prayed for with such fervor.

My bedroom's Hollywood bed and flowered yellow armchair were complimented by a cardboard bureau wallpapered in bouquets of pink roses. It held virtually anything one might imagine, ranging from hairpins to clothespins for the line that stretched from the windows to a distant pole, doilies, a few Christmas decorations, and a set of my paper dolls. In summer, the brown paper shades were drawn against the sun. In winter, the cool draft from the windows was delicious when felt from the warmth of wool blankets.

On twenty-four-hour duty in the kitchen beneath me, the Forestville shelf clock with its figurehead of a lady like the bowsprit of a ship counted minutes with a hearty tick and hours with a bong, a racket I interpreted as its message that all was well. As quiet as it was on our side of the wall, the neighbors' side was another story. If the voices rose to a certain pitch during quarrels, my grandmother would sometimes put a glass to the wall to see what was the matter. Grandpa frowned on this, so it could only happen if he was upstairs or in the yard. The glass Grandma favored for this was one from the Welch's grape jam collection with pictures of Howdy Doody and Clarabelle. In her felt slippers neatly slit on the side to accommodate her bunions, a seasonally appropriate apron tied over her dress, and one of the veiled hats she favored even for indoor use to cover her fine, straight hair that never took a curl to her satisfaction, my grandmother was in her element listening beneath the lithographs of Killarney's lakes as I kept lookout by the stairs for Grandpa.

On the other side of her door lay a landscape more rural than that of Willow Street. Beyond Rawley Avenue, farther than we would ever walk lay the East Mountain Reservoir, its name spelled out on its banks in flowers. After that came the hills of Prospect. On our walks in that direction, the route we took demonstrated the kind of variety in some city neighborhoods that would have given an out-of-towner the idea that Waterbury had no planning and zoning commission.

We passed a package store, the big home of an Italian family with a grape arbor, a Mom and Pop convenience store, the farmhouse of an Irish family whose horse grazed in the front yard, some triple-deckers and a tavern, some new little houses, and ended up at the new St. Joseph Cemetery at the corner of Pearl Lake Road. The old St. Joseph Cemetery held down the opposite end of Hamilton Avenue at Silver Street. In both the names were largely Irish, the markers simple stones punctuated by an occasional angel or member of the Holy Family.

We sometimes dallied in the cemetery or stopped to watch the neighbor's horse, but we always made time to stop into the Saxe and Floto Florist on our return trip along the opposite side of the street. A green wooden door with a wide glass pane was flanked by twin picture windows. It led to a dim, seldom-used front room. Most customers preferred to use the side entrance down a path that led toward a huge boulder shaped vaguely like a saddle.

In the florist's back room that was the true heart of the operation sat Grandma's friend in a cotton smock at her desk, surrounded by stacks of long white cardboard boxes and spools of pastel ribbons, clay pots, and the colored foil papers to wrap them. Beyond that room and on either side of it, the dozen or so greenhouses fanned out seemingly for miles. Sun streamed through their windowpanes like the rays in the opening credits of the soap opera *Guiding Light*. I could count on our visit to last at least half an hour, so after I'd said hello, I felt free to drift off to tour the greenhouses.

I'd never paid much attention to Grandma's garden, a tiny patch of marigolds and zinnias along the walk to her door, except for when the Japanese beetles paid their annual visit. Then Grandpa and I placed bets on how many of them we could count on a single flower. But being in the Saxe and Floto greenhouses made me think that one day I might give gardening a try.

In each of the glass houses, long wooden tables held potted plants and seedlings. Moist air from the sprinkler system mixed with the scent of geraniums, chrysanthemums, and potting soil. I could feel the air around me as soft as the cloak in *The Little Lame Prince* that his godmother had given him to keep him company.

The lushness of the flowers in full bloom and the luxuriant warmth made a good background for the family of tawny cats that called the florist home. They sunbathed and slunk around like jungle cats in a *Tarzan* movie. Shadrach, a massive patriarch with seven toes on each foot, favored the rim of the fieldstone goldfish pond someone had built in the greenhouse nearest to the office. The carp there were far larger than I'd ever imagined those gold and white fish in Woolworth's tank could grow. I leaned against the stones, Shadrach beside me, and watched them circle in and out of the lily pads to sink in a leisurely way to the depths below.

Behind the greenhouses, across the Mad River, lay Hamilton Park. Its rose gardens were extensive, laid out in row after row of multicolored beds punctuated by the occasional white trellised arch along the section that bordered Silver Street. Along with Carrie Welton's horse fountain and the train station's clock tower, the rose garden was one of the scenes most commonly photographed for postcards of Waterbury.

Although I hadn't been around to see it, I'd been told that Hamilton Park had once had a small zoo complete with monkeys and an owl. Nearly as interesting to me as the zoo might have been was the Victory House. Installed on a grassy bank above a pond with a spouting center fountain, the miniature, playhouse-sized white-columned mansion had stood on the Waterbury Green as the centerpiece of the Great War's Liberty Loan Drive. A second trip downtown had been necessary because of World War II when the house sold war bonds. After V-J Day and the end of the war effort, the little house retired.

Also, in retirement on the grounds of Hamilton Park were a rotting German cannon captured in the Great War and an equally decrepit water wheel from Waterbury's industrial past. Those relics made history come alive for me in a way that my schoolbooks' tidy facts never could have managed. Hamilton Park, like Hayden and Fulton, the parks I spent the most time in, had been given to the city by wealthy benefactors. Their gifts commemorated family names in a rather grand yet abstract way, quite the opposite of the artifacts housed downtown in the Mattatuck Historical Society's brick mansion across from the Green.

At least once each week on my way home from Notre Dame Academy, I visited the white portico mansion on East Main just beyond the Farrington building that housed the Mercy Boyd Bookstore. Inside the dimly lit front hall was a glass case with a display that included a pickled head garnered from some distant tribe that favored flattening skulls with a wooden vice. It gave no hint at all of the treasures just beyond in the main room. That room was Waterbury's attic.

Most fascinating of all the exhibits was Larry, the skeleton of a slave who'd either "jumped or been pushed into the Naugatuck River" and died. There was no mention on the information card of how or why Larry had been rendered into bones by his owner or denied burial. Not far from him stood the marble bust of a child with the wistful inscription Little Willie Lives in Heaven.

Beyond them was my favorite exhibit, a large cream-colored dollhouse complete with sweeping staircase and attic. It was fitted to scale with everything a real house might possibly need, from rugs and velvet draperies to a fireplace, bedroom suites to a maid's closet stocked with tiny mops and brooms. The museum also housed a black buggy once used by a local doctor to make his rounds and an unusually interesting marble statue of an angel with a wide wingspan swooping over a supine woman. This demanded close scrutiny because I could see that his wings were clearly detachable and if removed, would give the pair a completely different interpretation.

The museum's display cases were crammed with artifacts. There were lacy fans and tiny kid gloves, lightly worn dancing slippers, brass-buttoned Civil War uniforms, and wedding gowns that looked as if they'd been worn by children my age in days gone by. The things I saw provided an evolutionary time line for me in the same way as Grandma's Victorian table and fifties' couch. What I couldn't see, as I inspected the past from my postwar vantage point, was that the era I was living in in Waterbury during the relative quiet of the Eisenhower years was drawing to a close as well.

On Grandma's side of town, we lived in the shadow of Pine Hill at a time before Attorney John Grecco dreamed of erecting Holyland, USA, the Bible country village he constructed and crowned with a huge electrified cross. The rocky hill was covered in fall with a leafy red vegetation that looked to me like pictures I'd seen of Torc Mountain in Killarney. Grandma's sister was reputed to have climbed every mountain in Ireland except for Torc, the one in her own backyard. It occurred to me that our walks should be expanded to include mountains, as a legacy that deserved to be honored. Yet no matter how I coaxed her to climb Pine Hill, my grandmother always found a reason to decline.

If we had ever gotten to the top of Pine Hill, we'd have been treated to a view that was Waterbury as far as the eye could see: east, past Scovill's and Hamilton Park all the way to Calvary Cemetery; south to Saint Anne's Church and beyond to the Brooklyn section across the Naugatuck River; west to the towers of Our Lady of Mount Carmel Church in Town Plot; and north to Cracker Hill.

The city seemed enormous to me and what lay beyond its limits, a mystery to be solved. Sunday drives with Dad's parents took us to Woodbury for donuts from Phillips' Diner or to Bethlehem to the Regina Laudis Monastery to see its creche at Christmas or to buy the jellies and jams made by the nuns. In Watertown, we might stop for a Carvel or visit the rock next to the gazebo that had Grandpa's name on it for having served in World War I. And in December, a trip to Torrington to Santa's Christmas Village complete with deer, one with his nose reddened with Mercurochrome to look like Rudolph, was at the top of the travel destination list.

But though I enjoyed those trips past farms and fields of cows, the isolated big houses and the newer ranch houses in pastel colors never pleased me as much as Waterbury's energetic diversity did. I liked the city's sidewalks and smokestacks, the bustle of traffic and of people on the streets, and the cozy look of the lights in our neighbors' houses at dusk. Most of all, I liked the train station's brick clock tower, and I looked forward at the end of our Sunday forays to my first glimpse of it in the distance because it meant that we were almost home.

Flood Friday

By August 18 in the summer of 1955, there had been so much rain that the mayor of Torrington declared a state of partial emergency. In Waterbury, preparations were in full swing for the world premier of Rosalind Russell's *Girl Rush*. Grandma had a new dress from Jones Morgan for the gala that Thursday night at the State Theater. White pique with black piping, the dress's row of faceted jet buttons glittered in the kitchen's overhead light as Grandpa peered out the window at the rain.

My grandfather was the designated chauffeur of the evening, scheduled to drive Grandma and two of his sisters who lived in Brooklyn. Even the mayor was going to *Girl Rush* to give the welcoming speech to Waterbury's own movie queen. We turned on the front porch light and stepped outside. Houses on the other side of the street looked indistinct. The few cars that headed up or down Willow plowed water into waves that rolled back on themselves. They crested and broke against the sidewalks' curbs.

Grandma's pleas were no match for Grandpa's weather eye. His green Chevy stayed in our backyard that night, and Grandma stayed home with us. Grandpa's sisters got a ride with a neighbor and phoned later to tell about the premier and the water they'd waded through to reach the State's glass doors.

Next morning, I awoke to the sound of our tiny transistor radio turned up loud. There was no other sound as my mother and grandmother sat at our kitchen table listening. The day was Black Friday, the morning of the flood that had left the whole Naugatuck Valley a disaster area. Below us at the bottom of Willow Street, boats motored along Freight Street attempting rescue missions and searching for survivors.

No water came from the kitchen tap when I turned it on, and our electricity was gone as well. But oddly enough, we still had our phone.

"Gone," Grandma repeated into the black receiver of the wall phone at news of the three-family house where she'd raised my father. The report that rushing water could pick up and carry away a house the size of that four-square, triple-porched, three-family fortress seemed impossible. It was like a Grimm fairy tale where castles and the treasures in them vanished with a sorcerer's single gesture or secret word.

At the State Armory on Field Street, the Red Cross set up a base for emergency flood relief. Waterburians were advised to report for typhoid vaccinations. I stood with my mother and grandmother in a long line that snaked back upon itself up Field Street past the piazza of city hall. The people waiting in the line were very quiet.

Overhead, helicopters beat their way through the hot sky, bringing supplies to Waterbury Hospital on the west side of the river. All the rest of the summer into early fall, my father and grandfather were gone for days at a time, traveling with emergency crews along the path of the Naugatuck, restoring telephone service and electricity to whatever the flood had left standing. When they did come home—tired, dirty, and grim—they talked in low voices after I was in bed about what they'd seen.

I'd grown up on easy terms with the river and Brooklyn. They were part of my history. My dad's grandfather, a carpenter, had built his family home at 619 Riverside Street. My dad had lived on the top floor as a boy with his parents and brother and sister in four small rooms with gabled ceilings. That third-floor rent figured in one of my favorite stories. Tired of walking his dog up and down three flights of stairs that zigged like Zorro's *Z*, Dad had rigged a harness with some of his mother's clothesline and lowered Brownie down for his constitutional.

Many of Dad's stories sounded like adventures from *The Hardy Boys* novels. He'd hunted river rats with a BB gun, skated on the river during one especially cold winter, found a garnet ring after a flood and given it to his sister. He'd played the fife in the St. Joseph's school band, visited the train's roundhouse, ridden the Riverside Cemetery's workhorse one night after dark.

"And when there was a flood, if it looked as if the water was going to come into the house, my aunt and uncle on the first floor rolled up the rugs and stacked things on the tables," Dad explained.

"Then they'd come upstairs, and we'd watch from the back porch." People who lived along the river's banks took flooding as a matter of course.

The Naugatuck lay behind my family's house, at the rear of a wall of gray garages, beyond a chain link fence. No visit was complete, as far as I was concerned, unless I walked back there to pitch a few rocks into the swiftly flowing water. It seemed a long way down to the bottom of the steep embankment before the rock landed with a satisfying splash.

On the Sundays that we went to Mass at St. Patrick's on Charles Street, we'd stop in afterward for visits with Grandpa's three sisters and his brother. The family resemblance among them was strong in their thick white hair and deep-set brown eyes. Like Grandpa, none of them was tall, but they all had a reserved manner that made our visits seem ceremonial.

One great-aunt lived on the first floor with her husband, their daughter, her daughter's husband, and their two children. Their kitchen was larger than our living room, and I often thought that its pantry with glass-doored cupboards would make a great playhouse. Toll House cookies were that aunt's forte, served with pale, fizzy locally made Diamond ginger ale. I felt sophisticated to be sitting in their house still in my Sunday hat and gloves, sipping soda before noon.

The household on the second floor included another great-aunt, her husband, my widowed great-uncle, and my great-great-aunt. The level of perfection of this aunt's housekeeping was said by my grandmother to be because she was childless, a fact I found exotic. In her sunny rooms, the lace curtains stood at attention. The mahogany tabletops gleamed. And the Royal Doulton ladies dancing on the whatnot shelves held their positions where they'd been placed to best advantage.

The third floor was home to a widowed great-aunt, her two sons, and a cousin. This cousin was a man with a tattoo of an American eagle on one arm, its details colored in blue and red. There were a lot of people in that one house, but it didn't seem unusual. All along the gently curving street that hugged the river's bank were multifamily houses with as many or more in each. Backyards were deep. Many had rows of garages, or the occasional barn for a long-gone horse. One bigger barn was home to Paul's Soda, a local staple at weddings and graduations that came in a rainbow of flavors and was usually served by placing the bottles on ice in a galvanized washtub.

Across the street from my family's house was Riverside Cemetery. Twin gates in the black iron fence opened onto a huge urn with two seated statues. Behind this lay a small pond, and above that, a second one. The pond had swans, one of them black, and none too friendly. On our walks there, Grandma and I admired them from a safe distance. To the right of the entrance stood a stone chapel with steep spires and a porte cochere. The cemetery was hushed and lovely, and neighborhood people used it as a park, sitting in the shady green oasis on hot summer afternoons or strolling its hilly paths beneath tall shade trees.

At the top of one rise was a bench of iron lace, cut out in a pattern of flowers. Unlike Catholic cemeteries where statues of Jesus, Mary, or angels were the norm, Riverside's monuments were crowned with life-sized statues of Civil War soldiers at ease, longhaired women in flowing robes, and even an elk on a rough-hewn granite base.

"Yet shall he live," wrote the bronze figure of a young woman crouching before a tomb. Carrie Welton, whose horse, Knight, overlooked the Green, was at Riverside as well as many people whose names I recognized from the signs on Waterbury's streets. It was clear that these dead had been the city's elite.

In the time before we moved to Cracker Hill, my dad's parents lived across from the family homestead at the corner of Riverside and Summit, and my mother and I often walked down Washington Avenue to visit. Grandma's landlady lived on the floor above her, and so it seemed as if the backyard and its imposing white hydrangea bush was mostly ours. To divert me from pursuing the landlady's tabby cat, Grandma hung a swing in the doorway of the long back hall. The entry's darkness was a perfect foil for the brightness of the hydrangeas framed in the wavy glass of the back door's small glass panes.

From the front porch of Grandma's house, I could see an apartment block sided in peeling asphalt shingles made to look like brick. In the building was a canvas shop that made awnings, and above it, in one small apartment, an old lady who made little baskets out of greeting cards by crocheting them together. I loved those baskets, the cards cut into squares with holes punched at intervals in their sides. The colored threads joined "happy birthday" to "season's greetings" in a cheerful mix of sentiments. In warm weather, Grandma's neighbor worked at her open window, calling out greetings in Lithuanian to neighbors passing by, her white braids wound around her head like a crown.

The Brooklyn section of Waterbury was a little village of its own. You could get everything from gasoline to groceries without leaving the city's snug southwest corner. Brooklyn had both St. Patrick's Church where I'd been baptized and St. Joseph's where you could hear Mass said in Lithuanian. The windows at St. Patrick's told the life of the saint in stained glass. My own favorite depicted an ornately garbed Patrick driving the snakes out of Ireland. An amethyst-faced Gorgon with limbs of purple snakes writhed away from the emerald green-cloaked saint as he pointedly showed the way out with a gesture of his golden crook.

Brooklyn had its own movie theater and a branch of the Silas Bronson Library located just up the street from the newsstand where we supplemented our Waterbury news with the New York *News* and *Mirror*. There was a clothing store where Grandpa had once bought me a striped pinafore when I'd complained that I'd gotten my dress dirty, a drugstore where Dad had found my gray plush cat with glass eyes that we called the "green-eyed monster," a tailor, a shoemaker, and around the corner on John Street, the Brooklyn Bakery, the neighborhood's fragrant heart.

At night on weekends, customers could walk down the alley beside the shop to the bakery's back door. Inside, flour-dusted bakers in white uniforms and caps shoveled loaves of round dark rye and pumpernickel into and out of the wall of brick ovens using long-handled wooden paddles. Dad had a friend at the bakery from St. Joseph's school days who always greeted him with an enthusiasm that included me.

"Hello, my good friend, Bobby," he'd say, beaming. And if things were slow, he'd sometimes invite me to work the press that squirted red jelly into the centers of the donuts. Once filled, they were laid out in rows on a white table in the center of the big warm room.

It seemed impossible that much of Brooklyn had been swept away, unimaginable that the Naugatuck River had risen past the top of its steep banks, past the height of the train trestle at the corner of Riverside and Washington streets. It was horrible to think that whole houses with people still in them had disappeared in the swirling water. The house my great-grandfather had built was one of them, lifted up from its foundation and broken against the wreckage of Ward's flats.

We heard from the great-aunt and great-uncle who'd lived on the first floor of how they'd stayed behind with their son-in-law to set rugs and furniture out of harm's way while the rest of the family had left. The water rose at an alarming rate, entering the house. They decided to go upstairs to the second floor. The family there was on vacation, and they'd joked among themselves about the trouble they'd be in if they didn't replace the pane of glass they'd had to break to get the door open.

The water kept rising. On the third floor, they were let in by the cousin who'd been asleep. The house began to move, turning on its foundation so that its back porches that had faced the river now faced the cemetery and Riverside Street. The four of them went up into the attic. They broke through a skylight, and standing on suitcases and boxes of Christmas ornaments, they helped each other out onto the slate roof, where they held onto the chimney as the house floated away.

My great-aunt and great-uncle were rescued when the house hit the train trestle, but the two cousins were not so fortunate. They drowned on Black Friday, one of them identified weeks later only because of his tattoo. To commemorate the flood of 1955 the Waterbury *Republican-American* published a book of photographs. *Western Connecticut's Great Flood Disaster* was its title. Several of the photos showed our family's house in its last hours. The curtains were drawn, the family members inside nowhere in sight. Other photos showed men rigging lines to houses where people waved frantically from upstairs windows and men in boats with outboard motors tying up to porches and roofs to rescue whomever they could find.

"Why couldn't those rescue boats save our family?" I asked my father. "Why didn't they call for help?" And most important of all, "Why didn't they leave while they still had the chance?"

I wanted him to give me reasons that would make sense of August 19. I wanted answers that would rule out things you couldn't guard against, things like bad luck or bad timing or fate. But I found no reassurance in Dad's simple explanation.

"They didn't leave because the Naugatuck River had never risen that high before," my father said.

"No one imagined that anything like this could happen."

Christmas

It was Christmas that capped each year, and the anticipation of the holiday was as much of a thrill for me as the actual event. One sign that made its coming official was a discrete admonition on the front page, lower right hand corner, of the Waterbury newspaper alerting all citizens that it was time to begin preparations. Set off in a border embellished with bells and holly was the notice: Only—More Shopping Days Until Christmas.

The paper's clarion call got the season moving. At that time, Connecticut had something called blue laws. Stores were closed on Sundays, and one day less each week in the retail calendar meant that the days left dwindled more rapidly.

December 1 was the day I taped my annual Advent calendar to the refrigerator door. I favored the secular version, with jolly Santa loading his sleigh with toys or overseeing the elves hard at work at the North Pole. Holy versions usually featured a panoramic view of Bethlehem's hills and houses by night with shepherds and wise men shielding their eyes as they approached the blinding brightness of the star above the manger.

In both versions, tiny scenes were hidden within the big picture behind little doors. You'd get up close, squint to find the day's number cleverly concealed beneath Santa's beard or a camel's backpack, and pry open the flap to see the picture or quote underneath. If I had the kitchen to myself, I'd open as many as I could, smoothing the paper doors back to avoid detection.

All along Willow Street, houses began sporting wreaths and window decorations and strings of electric lights, and our drugstore counters filled with boxes of Christmas cards and gift-bowed perfume sets. But the real tip off to the season at our house was the ease with which the Sears Roebuck Catalogue fell open at the toy section. Sears was Santa's helper. In my eyes, it was as good as Dad's AAA map, the guide to the ultimate holiday destination underneath the Christmas tree.

Although my taste was firmly established, I always looked through all the offerings for clues to what my peers might fancy. Many toys were child-sized models of grown-ups' tools and appliances. The Junior Homemaker Kitchen Set, for example, was comprised of a stove, sink and matching refrigerator in pale pink. It came with plastic pork chops done to a turn and a handily prefrosted cake risen to perfection.

For practice for future glamorous nights on the town, there was the Little Miss Dress Up—which included a faux lipstick, a feathered boa, and a jeweled tiara. Clearly, that outfit would require a special occasion in Waterbury, perhaps the Policemen's Ball at the State Armory. My grandmother had taken me there once to watch Grandpa's sister and her policeman husband dance to an orchestra as we sat admiringly in the balcony on wooden benches.

Unlike real babies, the doll babies were tractable and sweet with eyes that closed when you wanted them to and stayed that way. Once I'd gotten one that wet when you fed her bottled water. Not content with that, I fed her sliced bologna and waited for the result that never came. After the doll had sat in the sun all one day, it was necessary for Dad to surgically remove her meal. The dolls I received after that were smooth plastic with no openings. The shiny tin dollhouses with perfectly color-coordinated furniture for each room had rugs, draperies, and pictures stamped permanently on their walls and floors and looked like a way to have things, at least in miniature, exactly the way you'd like them. Oddly enough, the houses never included a box of plastic people to live in them. Inhabitants were left to the individual owner's discretion.

In the fifties, it was possible to order even pets from Sears. I'd been told, "Forget it!" about the Shetland pony and the Lassie look-alike collie pup, but anything else, except for the Junior Chemistry Set and the Daisy .22 rifle, were fair game for my list. During the year, we lived on a budget, but at Christmas, my wishes usually came true.

Payday came on Thursday for much of Waterbury, and to accommodate shoppers, the stores downtown stayed open until 9:00 p.m. It was a common practice to pay bills in person at the stores, and on occasions when my mother or grandmother took me along, I found the crowded streets exciting. We'd stroll down Bank Street in the dark, looking into the brightly lit windows dressed for Christmas. Gilded branches and angel hair snow, boxes wrapped in colored foils with gold bows, and mannequins dressed in the latest fashion in hues of green or red whetted shoppers' appetites. Music was everywhere, from faint carols wafting out of Worth's glass doors to the louder sounds of the Salvation Army's speakers set up by its donation kettle in front of Howland-Hughes. Bundled up and bustling, the crowd with their mysterious bags and boxes were purposeful and full of energy. I got a heady sense of routines suspended for the duration of the season.

Santa himself was downtown on a golden throne banked in clouds of angel hair, his white beard hooked firmly behind his ears. On call both in Worth's children's section where the photographer had his studio and in Howland-Hughes's basement level toy section, he seemed omnipresent and as unnerving as if God himself had shown up at ten o'clock Mass.

"Have you been good this year?" he'd boom to the children seeking his lap, provoking an equal amount of confidences and tears. The explanation for multiple Santas, in the years when I hovered between belief and doubt, was that the men in red were helpers hired by busy Santa to collect the good children's wish lists. There was always an elf holding the velvet rope that separated him from the crowd of expectant lined up children, and to have a photo taken with Santa was only $2.99. During December, my mother sometimes rather pointedly sang a song called "Santa Claus Is Coming to Town." Its chorus went this way:

> He sees you when you're sleeping!
> He knows when you're awake!
> He knows if you've been bad or good!
> So be good for goodness's sake!

It was a song that brought me up short as Grandpa would've put it. What was Santa after all? A jolly old elf, as the poem said, or a nosy hogan with a bent for revenge in the gift department? This holiday duality was something I'd noticed before, with Easter for example, an annual event that included both the Easter Bunny and the Crucifixion. I wondered if I was the only one who thought about these things.

"For Pete's sake, it's just a song!" my mother explained. But it made me think of a doll my best friend had had that was Little Red Riding Hood on one side, yet with a flip of the skirt it became the Big Bad Wolf beneath.

We agreed to think of other songs, ones about reindeer and snowmen, and to focus on the gifts we'd choose to give to someone else. Unlike other holidays, Christmas was about secrets and the element of surprise. At school, what to get our families was as big a topic as what we wanted ourselves. And although my final selections were fairly predictable, making out my list gave the proposed shopping excursion an air of adventure as I printed a question mark after each listed item to allow for last-minute inspiration.

My first stop was the Waterbury Savings Bank, a gray stone fortress at the bottom of North Main Street where I'd built up my Christmas Club to twenty-five dollars, accumulated at fifty cents a week. Inside, I crossed the marble floor to a wall of filigreed iron cages that separated customers from tellers. This gave me a sense of security about my savings. My grandparents had lived through the Great Depression and always kept some money hidden in their house in case the banks failed again. But I trusted that palace and imagined my quarters nestling safely in a velvet-lined vault, waiting for me to collect them in December.

My next stop was always Howland-Hughes's notions department where Christmas aprons were a good bet for my grandmothers, in glamorous shades of red and gold chiffon. There, too, were the linen handkerchiefs for my father. On the first floor of the store were other great ideas: Christmas corsages with holly and tiny bells, costume jewelry brooches to suit every pocketbook, manicure sets in leatherette cases, and once a box of tall matches printed on all four sides with a firehouse scene that resembled Engine Six at the top of Willow.

Woolworth's was where I shopped for the final holiday touches: a box of Christmas cards to give out in class, a toy for my sister, perfume for my mother from the same counter where her mother bought the intriguing cobalt blue bottles of Evening in Paris cologne, and last but not least, catnip mice for our cats. Woolworth's was my own equivalent of catnip at any time of year but, especially so in December, favoring flash as I did in holiday decor. I gloried in the displays of Shiny Brite tree ornaments and tinsel garlands, plaster manger sets, and Santa lapel pins with red noses that lit up when you pulled the little string beneath them.

Dad's mother on the second floor of our house shared my enthusiasm. Her windows gleamed with plastic candelabra, four different colored bulbs to each. Grandma's silver tree was spotlighted with a wheel that revolved—coloring the tree blue, red, green, or orange in sequence. Beneath the tree lay a life-sized plaster baby Jesus wrapped in a receiving blanket and laid in a wooden doll's cradle with a tiny blue lamb on its headboard.

Brought down from the attic to its place between the two front windows was a cardboard fireplace with a little light behind its cardboard logs. If our house had ever had real fireplaces, they were long gone by the time we lived there, so I found this one with its bright red printed bricks a treat. There was a tin wheel that revolved from the heat of the lightbulb behind the logs and gave them an amber glow. And warmed by the idea of fire on cold December nights, I looked out on cars crunching their way uphill, the heavy chains on their tires providing traction in the snow.

Our tree downstairs was the traditional real pine, with strings of night-light-sized multicolored bulbs that burned hot enough to melt crayons, a fact I knew for sure because I'd tried it. Underneath its branches, the three wise men on foot inched their way toward the cardboard manger. We kept the camels down to three and the ox and donkey to one each, but I found the little sheep irresistible and added a few each year to the flock. The cellophane-wrapped package of fresh manger straw we spread out on the manger's floor beneath the Holy Family magnetized our cats. We'd see them skulking through the living room to crouch, tails thrashing, as they playfully cuffed a sheep or a shepherd out of the scene.

Each morning's mail brought a new supply of Christmas cards through the mail slot in our front door. My mother taped them up around the doorways and up the stair's banisters for added color. My favorite cards were the ones encrusted with glitter. My least favorites were the ones from our relatives in Ireland. These showed shakily painted Nativity scenes with a notation on the card that read "painted by mouth by Tim" or more frightening yet, "painted by foot by Tom." Who knew what catastrophe had crippled those poor artists? I was sure that in their place, I'd never make the grade as they had, having tried once in private with no success.

School was easier in December because whole chunks of our day were spent cutting out construction paper bells and candles to tape to our classroom windows and bulletin boards. In the school's entrance hall, an empty manger was set up along side a bale of hay. The idea was that every time a girl did a good deed, she could add a straw to the manger, and by December 25, baby Jesus would have a soft bed.

Rehearsal for the annual Christmas pageant went into high gear, and the entire school participated. The pageant I remember best found us all lined up according to grade, in sets of two. We marched into the darkened auditorium carrying flashlights. At the count of three, we all turned them on underneath our chins, blinding ourselves, as we sang, "O come, o come, Eee-ma-ha-ahn-u e-l . . ." Every year my father offered to pay double for his ticket if he could just stay at home, but I couldn't wait for the show. Secretly I dreamed of a Hollywood talent scout in the audience waiting to discover me and whisk me out to California to a spot on *The Mickey Mouse Club* show.

Holiday clothes were unbeatably glamorous. For the flashlight show, we'd worn quilted red taffeta circle skirts that swished as we walked. They were buoyed up by at least one crinoline half slip in ruffled crackling tiers. The more affluent girls, though not always the thinnest, wore three or four slips at once, their skirts flounced out like tutus. Those outfits were in reaction, I think, to the previous year's entertainment, where we'd all been dressed as poor orphans. We'd had to go to Lerner's to buy blue maid's uniforms, and our parents hadn't liked that one bit.

"We're not sending our daughter to Notre Dame Academy to be a housemaid," more than one parent had told our principal.

Dresses for Friday-night dancing school weren't costumes, strictly speaking, but I spent so much of my time in uniform that they seemed so. In Waterbury, there were two schools for ballroom dance, Miss Coffee's and Mrs. Reems's. Miss Coffee's students were drawn from what my neighbor called the creme de la creme of local society. They met weekly in the grand ballroom of the Elton Hotel on the Green.

The rest of us went to Mrs. Reems's class in the auditorium of the Women's Club on Central Avenue. In that chilly brick citadel, her daughter pounding away valiantly on an upright piano, perhaps hoping by sheer volume to sound like a band, we learned the steps to the fox-trot, counting, "Step. Close. Step close. One." We then moved on to rumba to the tune of "Hernando's Hideaway," and to execute a step identified as the "ball and chain" for a dance that Mrs. Reems called the bop.

When we were judged sufficiently proficient, our families were invited to watch us at a formal dance. Whatever the season, my outfit for this was the same, a white chiffon gown my dad's mother had commissioned from a dressmaker who had her shop on the ground floor of the Trinity Apartments. The magic of the dress, according to its maker, was its versatility. Just by changing the sash, I could have a whole new look. The lavender sash was okay as it simply went around my waist to tie in back in a huge bow. But the other two, the red one and the green one, made me cringe. They draped from the right shoulder to the waist, then flared out to the gown's hem. Red was for Valentine's Day, Grandma said, and green was Christmas, together with a headband of velvet holly leaves.

It was bad enough that I'd entered my chubby era at this time, and even worse that the sashes made me look like Queen Elizabeth in her coronation photo. I knew exactly how the queen looked because my mother had an autographed photo of her. It had come to Willow Street in exchange for a birthday card my mother had sent to England. It was a fact that my Welsh-born mother had the same name and birthday as the queen, and a family joke that ever since my mother was little girl, my grandfather had often remarked that the stork had dropped the wrong baby that day at Buckingham Palace. There was no way out of wearing the sashes, and I went to my fate on Central Avenue like a condemned man to the gallows on sash nights.

Any Friday was made better by a trip to Pickett's Drugstore after dancing class for Cokes served in the booths at the back of the store. For formals, it was a trip to the Farm Shop on Watertown Avenue, driven by willing parents who waited patiently as we spooned our ice cream sundaes. But despite the green sash on my gown, the Christmas dance was the best one because it meant that school vacation was coming soon.

"We're looking down the jaws of Christmas now!" was the way my grandfather put it, heralding the arrival of the annual tree cut down and brought to the Waterbury Green. Hung with colored ornaments the size of basketballs and secured upright with guy wires tied to stakes, it held its own against the wreathed war memorial and the garlanded clock and Carrie Welton Fountain. Part of Grandpa's job as a park foreman was decorating the Green, and I looked forward to seeing him there, puffing on his pipe filled with Rum & Maple tobacco as I waited to catch the Overlook bus home.

The street department handled the foil candy canes on downtown's lampposts as well as the greetings strung across Bank Street and East Main that wished all a "Merry Christmas" in silver and red. Some neighborhoods went all out at Christmas as a group effort. Bunker Hill had an annual competition, and after the winner had been declared, we'd take a ride one night across town to see the best and brightest.

Some people outlined their whole houses in multicolored lights. Many had reindeer on their front lawns, led by Rudolph, his nose blinking red. My favorites had Santa himself on the roof, spotlighted on his way down the chimney with a sack of toys. On Cracker Hill, most people were content to place the tree in a front window or to substitute a more traditional front door wreath for a plastic smiling Santa face.

Above us on the boulevard, in a discrete nod to the season, single candles glowed white in front windows, with perhaps the glimpse of a tree toward a drawing room's rear corner on the silent, well-kept street.

In some ways, the anticipation of Christmas was better than the actual event, the unopened, brightly wrapped mystery as opposed to the reality of pajamas or socks from well-intentioned distant relatives who didn't know us well enough to gauge our sizes. Those stayed beneath the tree, gathering the gently falling needles as we read our Christmas books and steeled ourselves for the writing of thank you notes.

Visiting was a part of the season, and I looked forward to seeing other people's trees and sampling their cookies, particularly the Italian ones called *anginettes*. Because I spent a lot of time with my grandparents, I visited their friends too. Dad's mother had a girlhood friend who lived on Spring Lake Road at the end of an unpaved drive lined with pines. The tiny brown-shingled house smelled of kerosene from its parlor stove, the main source of heat. In the kitchen, the sink had a hand pump like something I'd seen in Western movies. There were curtains in the doorways instead of doors and no indoor plumbing. Grandma's description of chamber pots had been informative, but manners prevented me from asking to use the real McCoy.

On Christmas morning while our turkey roasted itself at 350 degrees, my grandparents took her a pot of soup. This was Grandma's Christmas recipe for chicken rice soup with a clear tomato broth. I'd go along, the heavy lidded cauldron wedged between my zip front arctic boots. The door was always opened by the old lady's brother, dressed in red suspenders. There was no Christmas tree in their house, but in the backyard, suet hung from an apple tree on a red string.

"It's for the birds' Christmas, honey," Grandma's friend from the thread-mill days explained. I wondered what it would be like to live as she did. The house was cozy with a feeling of having stepped back in time, the red checkered tablecloth giving it the ambiance I'd read about in Laura Ingalls Wilder's *Little House on the Prairie*.

It was light-years away from the feeling I'd gotten from a visit with my mother to a woman she'd known when she was small. Holidays were a time for honoring old ties, and this was a bond of gratitude on my mother's part. Mom sometimes told stories of her childhood that were sad enough to make me cry and were perhaps told to make me count my blessings. The woman we visited had been kind and attentive to her, and I knew that it was because of this that we visited, to return the favor.

Mom's friend lived on the second floor of a gray house out east. She, too, had a kerosene stove with a long metal pipe that disappeared into the blackened ceiling of the parlor, a cold room with a linoleum rug laid over the wooden floor. In a rocking chair drawn up close to the heat sat her father with his little dog.

"Have a candy," Mom's friend urged, holding out a box of chocolates that looked the worse for wear. My mother declined, frowning at me to do the same. Along with the smell of kerosene was the pungent smell of the open quart bottle with four roses on its label set out on the table and in her glass.

It was a scent I recalled from the previous summer when we'd met the lady downtown on Bank Street. My mother and I had been coming out of Worth's. I'd been wearing a navy blue dress with a red polka-dotted bow. We'd looked up to see my mother's old mentor weaving toward us, arms linked with a man in a rumpled suit. Her brown eyes were shiny, her speech slurred as she made the introductions.

"I could see by your uniform that you go to private school," the man told me. My mother pressed my hand to warn me not to point out his mistake in my attire.

"Come see me," the woman called to my mother as they went their way.

"What's wrong with them?" I asked. Seeing them had made me afraid with the sudden knowledge that grown-ups could veer so far off course.

"Never mind," Mom answered in the tone that meant no further discussion. Then to herself she added, "She could have been anything she wanted to be." And with a sigh, my mother guided me toward the Green to catch the bus for home.

If Christmas at our house meant decoration, then the holiday at Mom's parents' house was Noel in spades. Both grandmothers as well as my mother shared a taste for Christmas corsages, but Mom's mother was the only one of them who wore hers even indoors, pinned to her housedress. Both grandmothers wore holiday aprons too, but my mother's mother set hers off with a festive hairnet dotted with tiny sparkly jewels. And so it was no wonder that their house on Rawley Avenue was equally resplendent.

Grandma saved all her decorations, adding to them and rarely throwing anything away. Her cupboards and drawers were layered like the strata diagram marked What Lies Beneath Us in my picture book about planet Earth. Digging down, I could tell how far past Christmas we'd come by the depth of the cardboard Santa face and sprigs of velvet holly sunken beneath the Valentine's Day red hearts and St. Patrick's Day shamrocks in the sideboard drawer. I was especially fond of the silver foil bells hung in all the windows, the beaded garlands strung across the doorways, and the sight of Grandma kneading Irish soda bread at the kitchen table while Grandpa lighted his pipe with a wooden kitchen match of the type Dad called "barn burners" and pretended to advise.

Despite the fact that they lived in a housing project and we went there in Dad's Ford, Currier and Ives's "Home for Christmas" is what I pictured when we set out for our visit. Dad was a big fan of those pictures, and we'd collected a series of metal cans with copper lids bearing assorted scenes, courtesy of all the Red Rose tea we drank. The Christmas can, our most recent one from the A&P, had captured my imagination. On it a sleigh full of well-wrapped travelers were pulling up to a yellow farmhouse through deep snow. On its porch, a gray-haired couple waited, the pleasure of their anticipation engraved as plainly as our own.

Although easygoing in most things, Dad held fast to the tradition of his mother's Christmas soup and turkey stuffed with crackers. And so it was afternoon before we headed across town along Hamilton Avenue.

"Over the river and through the wood, to Grandfather's house we go," sang my mother as we passed Scovill's gritty brick walls. We'd memorized that poem by Lydia M. Child in school, and it seemed, despite the fact that she'd composed it for the Thanksgiving holiday, just right for the occasion. In front of my grandparents' house, the wide lawn was filled with snowmen made by the neighborhood children and outfitted in cast-off caps and scarves. Outside Grandma's door at the end of a long set of steps was a lilac hedge planted by Dad with cuttings from our own tree, covered in lacy snow. A little gate kept their yard in a separate enclosure.

Grandma's holiday turkey rested in the kitchen on the ironing board beneath a linen dish towel. In the living room, a folding table stood covered with a cloth patterned in red bells and sprigs of holly. Every inch of the top was covered. A bowl of red grapes and oranges, all with far too many seeds for me, a box of Whitman's Sampler with a cross-stitch pattern stamped on its yellow background, and a bowl of mixed nuts still in their shells accompanied by a nutcracker and pick jockeyed for position with a plastic sleigh pulled by eight reindeer and driven by a tiny Santa. On either side of him was a candlestick and a guttering red candle.

This was one of the days when Grandpa was sure to remark,

"Ah, we're on the pig's back for sure." The pig's back was an Irish expression that meant we were in luck. It included the heavily tinseled tree crammed into one corner and all of the family—my uncle and his wife and my two cousins, my great uncle, my parents, sister, and me.

"Grandpa, tell us about when you lived in Ireland," I'd coax, poking the bottoms of the chocolates gently with the nutpick to avoid the ones filled with jelly. My grandfather needed very little urging to tell a story and advised me in private never to let a few facts stand in the way of making the story a good one.

While the grown-ups lingered over turkey sandwiches and tea, I'd crank up the Victrola and play a few waxy 78 records like "I'll Take You Home Again, Kathleen" or "Danny Boy" until my mother called to me to give it a rest. And when even the cat had begun to yawn and hunt for a place to snooze, we said good night and "safe home" and walked down to our cars with our gifts, guided by the bright street lights of the city.

A New Year

Supplies for New Year's eve appeared in Woolworth's windows on December 26. There were piles of green and gold foil top hats, silver tiaras with feathered plumes, bags of multicolored confetti, noisemakers by the box that unfurled when you blew into them, and even glitter encrusted banners wishing "Happy New Year" to herald the final celebration of the season.

Just inside the doors, stacked three deep on a narrow counter, lay the diaries. With padded leatherette covers in shades of red and blue and brown, they held the promise of unlimited possibilities, a New Year's grab bag of events that might prove worth recording. The diaries' fragile locks came with little golden keys, each one taped in the back of its book inside a brown paper packet.

The lines in the five-year diaries were very short and impossibly close together, unless you were a person who could write in code. The one year version was more accommodating, with a whole page for daily confidences. Each new year I imagined myself writing as eloquently as Anne Frank about my own adventures, hopes, and fears. Reality, though, produced entries such as the following:

> Went to school.
> Did homework.
> Fed cats.

Still, the potential a new diary represented made it worth buying one. The first page was always devoted to what Dad's mother called "turning over a new leaf." On it, I recorded my resolutions:

1. Be kind to all.
2. Don't complain about homework.
3. Don't talk back.

Number three about talking back was an attempt to be daring, at least in print. Talking back was as unheard of in our house as poodles sprouting wings. I wrote all my resolutions out with my Sheaffer's fountain pen using peacock blue ink and my best cursive handwriting, a challenge because I was left-handed and prone to smudge. The intensity I brought to my task made it seem as if I might somehow come up with a dramatic New Year's resolution or at least a novel one.

"Maybe you'd like to shovel snow this year," Grandpa might suggest on his way out the door although it was understood that outside jobs belonged to the men in the family in the same way that indoor ones were the province of the women. Those frigid winter evenings after a storm were beautiful in the pinky glow from the streetlamps as Dad and his father hand shoveled our driveway, piling heaps of snow in furrows that reminded me of pictures I'd seen of farmers' plowed fields.

Not even a blizzard could keep the New Year from arriving, and on Willow Street, we stayed up to watch Guy Lombardo and his Royal Canadians on TV until it was time for the ball to drop in New York City's Times Square. If I'd elected to stay at my mother's parents' house, the routine varied slightly in that Grandpa went up to bed while Grandma and I welcomed the New Year in.

What we wore were our bedclothes, my footed pajamas of early years segueing into fifties lounging pajamas made of some slinky synthetic fabric, the mandarin-collared top not nearly warm enough for the last night in December. The grandmothers wore nightgowns and robes, my mother's mother's robe embellished with her silver Tara brooch. That was a pin with a story. Grandma's father had designed the pin. It was round and wreathed in shamrocks. In its center were a stone tower, an Irish wolfhound, and a harp. There was a twin to Grandma's pin on the other side of the world in Ireland. Grandma's sister had it, and I knew that my grandmother thought of her often and wore the pin almost daily in a kind of homage to their connection.

On Rawley Avenue, we readied our toast for the first stroke of twelve, black cherry soda served in red checkered juice glasses with black Scottie dogs dancing along their sides. As the Forestville clock bonged out the hour, Grandma headed for the front door to let the New Year in. My job was to raise the living room window to let the old year out. Technically, it should have been ushered out the back door with more formality, but lacking a rear entry, we fell back on the adage that it was the thought, after all, that counts.

I imagined I could see those phantom years trading places in the cold air that blew through the house: the new one a baby in diapers, the old one a bent Methuselah with a long gray beard. Grandma and I made our wishes silently, looking out together through the glass panes of the front door. Down where Rawley Avenue met Hamilton, the snow beneath the streetlights looked as white as the blank pages of my new diary.

For a while after my grandmother switched off the porch light, we lingered there, watching the streetlights and the lights of the neighbors' houses glowing against the dark hills and sky. Waterbury's morning *Republican* would be arriving in a few hours with its predictable banner headline wishing a "Happy New Year." The lead stories would feature the latest city news: a photo of the first baby born in the new year, and society page accounts of what party-going revelers had done and worn the night before.

The horoscope column was de rigueur reading for predictions of what each sign of the zodiac could expect in the months ahead, exciting to read whether or not you actually believed it, and even the cartoon strips promised new twists ahead for their ongoing stories.

New Year's Day, I saw, was about possibilities, even if technically it was simply another twenty-four-hour day. But even though so many things about January 1 were a given, in Waterbury and on Cracker Hill, there was always room for a few surprises.

The End